JESUS HEALS TODAY

JESUS HEALS TODAY

But you will receive power
when the Holy Spirit has come upon you;
and you will be my witnesses

Acts 1:8

COSTANDI G. BASTOLI

© Costandi Bastoli 2020

All rights reserved. Except for quotations, no part of this book may be reproduced or transmitted in any form or by any means, electronic or mechanical, including photocopying, recording, uploading to the internet, or by any information storage and retrieval system, without written permission from the publisher.

Published by Parousia Media Pty Ltd
855 Old Northern Road
Dural, New South Wales, 2158
+61 2 9651 0375
www.parousiamedia.com

Printed in Australia

Editor: Marita Winters

Cover design by Colette Silva (née Bastoli)

Unless otherwise mentioned, Scripture quotations are from the New Revised Standard Version Bible, used with permission.

Having read this book, if you need prayer for healing or wish to share your experience, feel free to contact Costandi on: costabas@icloud.com

Endorsements

Costandi Bastoli has been quietly engaged in a wonderful healing ministry over many years. In this book, appropriately titled Jesus Heals Today, *he gives a wide range of testimonies of physical, emotional and spiritual healings. I trust it will be read widely, since in this secularised age our faith needs strengthening. Theories can be discounted, arguments can be disputed, but witness of life cannot be opposed. I recommend the book to all who are seeking to grow in faith and discover more deeply the love and power of Jesus our Risen Saviour and Lord.*

Fr Ken Barker MGL - Founder and Moderator, Missionaries of God's Love Priests, Canberra.

Costandi Bastoli has been conducting annual healing seminars and rallies in Mt Hagen, Papua New Guinea, since 2015. Hundreds of people have benefited from his ministry and those who worked with him were greatly encouraged. In his easy to read book, Jesus Heals Today, *Costandi bears witness to what he has seen and heard Jesus doing for His people here and elsewhere.*

I recommend this book wholeheartedly and am sure that whoever reads it will grow in their knowledge and trust in the Lord and His ways, experience the power of His healing love, and anchor their hope in Him.

Most Rev. Douglas William Young SVD – Archbishop of Mount Hagen, Papua New Guinea.

Jesus Heals Today *is a testament to the fact that Jesus is alive today and working miracles among the faithful. Jesus' healing did not stop when His earthly life ended. Rather, He commissioned His disciples, then and now, to carry on His mission in the world, to minister Jesus' healing touch, to show Jesus' care for those who are wounded, and to make people whole again.*

Costandi is a man of great faith. He has been gifted with a wonderful ministry of prayer, of preaching and teaching. His outreach to those to whom he ministers is lifelong, and this is evidenced by those who keep in touch with him to acknowledge his support when they needed it most, even if it is many years after the prayer took place.

I met Cosi in mid-1995 after I had been introduced to the Disciples of Jesus Covenant Community. We have been companions on the faith journey ever since. A small part of my story is included in the pages of Jesus Heals Today. *I could have filled many more chapters with reflections on how Cosi's ministry of Jesus' healing has touched my life, as I am sure could many others who have shared their testimony.*

As you are reading this book take great courage that Jesus' healing ministry continues today.

Mrs Marita Winters – a grateful recipient of God's healing love, Sydney.

Jesus heals. The Gospels give witness to healing as an essential aspect to the ministry of Jesus. Jesus heals today. This book is a witness to the healing action of Jesus in our day. The stories recounted in this book reveal the joy experienced by people who know that it was the mercy and power of Jesus who healed them of their afflictions. Experiencing healing was not just relief from their burden and suffering but revealed to them the personal love God has for them. The healing led to deeper faith, deeper trust in God and a desire to live the Christian life. The experience of healing changed the heart of the person. They cannot but live in grateful thanks to God and the desire to praise Him by the new way in which they live. That Jesus heals takes us to the heart of the Gospel which proclaims that God loves the world so much that He sent His only Son, not to condemn but to save. I recommend this book as testimony to the fact that Jesus continues to heal in our day.

Most Rev. Julian Porteous DD – Archbishop of Hobart, Tasmania.

In Jesus Heals Today *Costandi Bastoli has given us a rich and comprehensive compilation of true stories to do with divine healing today and clear instructions on charismatic gifts, with ample Biblical passages to illustrate and back up the stories and the teaching. In addition, the author provides us with an excellent account of the move of the*

Holy Spirit in our time and much else besides. This book is a useful contribution to the literature on the subjects it covers.

Rev. Fr John Rea SM – author of *Witness to Wonders* and *Proclaim with Wonders*, well-known for his healing ministry, New Zealand.

Contents

Acknowledgements   15
Foreword   19

PART ONE   23

1. How I experienced baptism in the Holy Spirit   27
2. Jesus healed me in many, many ways   33
3. How I was set free from the addiction to   39
   smoking cigarettes
4. He just keeps on surprising me   45
5. Patience and trust as God came through in   47
   the end...
6. Barbara found her father   51
7. Jesus continues to set the oppressed free   55
8. Untie that donkey, for I have use for it   59
9. When a healing does not come immediately!   65
10. From His fullness Grace received grace!   71

11. From fear to faith	75
12. From scepticism to certainty	81
13. Healings and visions in Magauto	85
14. Baptised at the River Jordan	89
15. Let the children come to me!	95
16. Healed and became an instrument of His merciful love	97
17. A love story: God and man	103
18. The peace of Christ came, and insomnia was gone forever	107
19. Bearing witness to the doctor	109
20. Car accident, whiplash and then what happened?	111
21. Freed from pain, sickness and rejection	115
22. How Mel was healed from menstrual complications	117
23. Vanessa was diagnosed with hydrocephalus and then a brain tumour. What happened next...	119
24. Signs and wonders - Port Moresby, 2011	121
25. Vivienne forgave her husband	127
26. The lame walk, the blind see, and the deaf and dumb hear and speak	129
27. The Lord hears the cry of the poor	141
28. A season of Pentecost at Mount Hagen!	145
29. From Islam to atheism, then God spoke to him in his own language!	153
30. Healings and a pleasant surprise at Port Moresby	159
31. A former Premier, chiefs, and businessmen rejoice in the presence of the Lord	163

PART TWO	173
32. The basic Gospel message – bridge illustration	175
33. Jesus our healer	179
34. How do we understand baptism in the Holy Spirit?	185
35. The charismatic gifts	195
36. Faith and the gift of faith	199
37. Gifts of healings	203
38. The gift of tongues	207
39. A word of knowledge	215
40. What is resting in the Spirit?	219
41. A prayer for miracles (Fr John Rea SM)	221
PART THREE	227
42. What is Catholic Charismatic Renewal?	229
43. The Disciples of Jesus Covenant Community	233
44. Summer School of Evangelisation	235
45. Light to the Nations	237
46. The Missionaries of God's Love priests and brothers	239
47. The Missionaries of God's Love sisters	243
48. Conclusion	247

Acknowledgements

I thank God for my parents, George and Clothilde Bastoli, who shared their faith with me. I am grateful for my Aunt Rose Bastoli, who baptised me when I was in danger of dying as I was born prematurely. I am thankful for many in Jerusalem who nurtured my faith, particularly the De La Salle brothers, Abouna Michel Sabbah (now Patriarch Emeritus), and the Young Christian Students Society.

I thank God for our popes, beginning with Pope St John XXIII, up to our present pope, His Holiness Pope Francis. They have followed the lead of the Holy Spirit, welcomed the Charismatic Renewal and taught us about the charismatic gifts. I am most grateful that our Lord gave me opportunities to meet Pope St John Paul II and shake his hand five times.

I thank our Lord for the Catholic Charismatic Renewal, River of Life Covenant Community, and the Disciples of Jesus Covenant Community who provided me with a faith environment.

Many people over the years have encouraged me to write and keep records of my experience in praying over people.

I recall that when I was struggling with the question of whether I should write this book or not, I met an African Franciscan priest, I think his name was Fr Adam. I was leading a pilgrimage, and we had just arrived at the shores of the Lake of Galilee. Fr Adam came to me and said in his deep voice, "Jesus says to you, feed my sheep". I smiled and said to him, "Yes, I know," thinking that he was pointing out to me that we were at the site of the Church of the Primacy of St Peter.

But he repeated, "Jesus says to you, feed my sheep". I said, "Yes, I am," thinking that I was sharing my knowledge with the pilgrims I was leading and the people I am privileged to teach in our community and its outreaches. But Fr Adam repeated a third time, "Jesus says to you, feed my sheep". After I reflected on our conversation I concluded perhaps the Lord was encouraging me to write this book.

I shared my thoughts with the chaplain for that pilgrimage, Fr Paul Ghanem OFM. He said to me, "If there is a book inside you, put it on paper". Thank you, Lord, Fr Adam and Fr Paul.

The teachings and ministry of Francis MacNutt (RIP), Sister Briege McKenna OSC, and Fr John Rea SM inspired me and taught me a lot. So did Fr Eugene Stockton, Fr Jack Soulsby SM (RIP), and many charismatic lay leaders such as Brian Smith (RIP) and Jeff Lawrence.

I am grateful to Philip and Jennie Ryall and Tony Bittar for their encouragement; to Brian Cook for his assistance, and to my dear wife Barbara who ministered with me, for her contribution to this book and for putting up with me as I've spent many hours preparing this book.

Finally, I am most grateful to Fr Paul Glynn SM, not only for his encouragement but also for his many pieces of advice and support, and for so kindly writing the foreword for this book.

Also, I am most thankful to Marita Winters for her encouragement and for volunteering to edit this book for me and for Colette Silva my talented daughter who spent many hours designing the cover and offering her invaluable graphic design expertise.

I am most grateful for all the brothers and sisters who gave me the privilege of ministering to them and for allowing me to share what the Lord has done for them.

I am also grateful for the people who spiritually and financially supported me in my mission work.

Foreword
Fr Paul Glynn SM

I am moved that such a fine friend as Costandi has asked me to introduce his book. I read the book with real joy. We've just celebrated Easter and read of the two travellers to Emmaus. They are thoroughly dejected by the execution of Jesus. They had come to believe he was the promised Messiah who would free Israel. Jesus joins the two ex-disciples but manages to hide his identity and begins quoting the Scriptures that proclaim that the Messiah will suffer greatly. The light is fading, and the two persuade Jesus to join them in an evening meal. He agrees, sits at the table, takes bread and blesses it. Their eyes are opened, but Jesus is gone. They said to each other, "Did not our hearts burn within us as he talked to us on the road?" I've often heard Costandi talk to the Covenant Community branch he leads, and I could see his heart burns as he explains the Scriptures. In reading his new book, his heart burns as he writes, and I found my heart burning as I read on.

Fr Yves Congar OP was a great modern theologian and lecturer, full of spiritual insights that set many hearts burning. He proved he was a holy man when a top Vatican official publicly condemned him and had his licence to teach theology revoked. Congar didn't perform angrily, pick up his Bible and go off in a huff. Later Pope John XXIII, who knew the mettle of the man, named him to the Commission preparing Vatican II documents. Congar later wrote that the greatest tragedy in 20th century Catholicism was the divorce in theological seminaries of the study of theology from the pursuit of holiness. There, surely lay hidden sinkholes that caused the clerical sins against minors that were betrayals wrecking young lives and the faith of many. Another great modern spiritual writer, Fr Hans Urs Von Balthasar is reported making a similar desperately sad statement.

Costandi's book gives very beautiful and accurate theological descriptions of the baptism in the Holy Spirit, and the other key elements of the Catholic Charismatic Renewal, but they are not dry-as-dust descriptions. They are his lived experiences and the source of his very joyful Christianity. He has not divorced theology from his quest for holiness, and his fruitful witness to holiness. Costandi was among the delegates at the worldwide gathering of the Catholic Charismatic Renewal in Rome, 2017. They heard Pope Francis zealously encourage, with great enthusiasm, the Renewal's way of modern witness. Francis zeroed in on two elements: evangelising and reaching out to the poor.

Costandi's book is very practical and an encouraging witness and response to the Holy Father, giving chapter and verse to the physical and spiritual healings that have taken place during Costandi's outreach to the far from affluent people in Papua New Guinea especially. Our Easter Mass readings have been full of physical healings through the hands of Christ's first apostles. Some of the healings of New Guineans who were unable to walk are mirror images of the cripple from birth, begging at the temple gate, who through Peter and John's intercession, was sent forth running and leaping. Peter, an ex-catechist in Mount Hagen, healed after Costandi and his team's prayers, jumped up and took off running down the hall, while the congregation shouted encouragement and cheered him and the Lord.

Acts 2:42-43 gives a kind of definition of the first Christians: "they devoted themselves to the apostles' instruction and the communal life, to the breaking of bread and the prayers. And a reverent fear overtook them all, for the apostles performed many signs and wonders". John's Gospel calls the miracles of healing done by Jesus 'signs' and sometimes 'works.' John 10:25 puts it: "Jesus answered, the works I do in my Father's name give witness in my favour", and in 10:38, "But if I do perform them, even though you put no faith in me, put faith in these works, to realise what it means that the Father is in me and I in Him".

Costandi sees great importance in the sometimes-questioned healing ministry, one of the charisms that Paul speaks of very clearly. Sadly, Jesus spoke of the ill will of some people who do not want to know the truth.

Something very attractive in Costandi's book is the healing of hearts, usually after he has led the sufferer to forgive the person(s) who wounded the sufferer. He has led many angry, deeply hurt people to go back to the cause and, following the words of the Our Father, and Jesus' seven times seventy times teaching, to forgive that person. Sometimes it takes some time, but Costandi has led many self-torturing souls, in our modern society where so many people are angry, resentful and deeply depressed, to the peace that comes from forgiving in the spirit of the Gospel. I have been helped by two Marist priests who have followed the Catholic Charismatic Renewal spirit that this new book explains so well. One was Dr John Thornhill, who was invited by the pope of the time to join the Roman International Commission of theologians. He joined the Catholic Charismatic Renewal and chose the name for the group I belonged to, Mary of Pentecost, that used to meet regularly in the packed parish church in Mary

Street, Hunters Hill, NSW. The other was Dr Jim Esler. As a layman, Jim won the gold medal as top law student at Sydney University. A future Australian Prime Minister was a fellow student with Jim. Jim was then invited to university lectorship in law but chose instead to join the Marist Seminary at Toongabbie, near Parramatta. Eventually sent to Rome to study Canon Law, he took out the gold medal there. Later he taught theology and spirituality in several seminaries as a much-loved teacher. He joined the Catholic Charismatic Renewal and became spiritual director at the Mary of Pentecost Community in Hunters Hill.

We sorely need evangelisers like Costandi Bastoli, with 'fire in their belly' as the old saying has it. Or, evangelisers 'who teach with unction', as was a beautiful expression when I was ordained back in 1953. The 'unction' means the anointing of the Holy Spirit. Jesus was anointed by the Holy Spirit, as Isaiah promised the Messiah would be, to bring good news to the poor, to make the blind see, to set people free. Pope St Paul VI once said moderns have become leery of 'teachers' because so many 'gurus' in modern days have been shown to be inauthentic. But, the pope added, people will listen to witnesses, and if people listen to a teacher, you will find he is also a genuine witness. May I recommend the teacher and witness, Costandi Bastoli, whose whole life, evangelising and healing ministry is based on the Scriptures, personal prayer, and community living with the Blue Mountains Covenant Community called the Disciples of Jesus. One great blessing in his life is a totally loving and dedicated wife and mother of their five children, Barbara, his life's partner until death, who reminds me of Ruth, King David's grandmother.

Fr Paul Glynn SM

PART ONE

"He sent them out to preach the kingdom of God and to heal the sick," (Luke 9:2).

Over 40 years ago, I experienced an encounter with the living Lord through 'Baptism in the Holy Spirit'[1]. I think of it as my personal Pentecost experience. I can divide my life now into before and after that experience. This experience made my spiritual life vibrant.

In my new life, I discovered the charismatic gifts[2]. I found myself teaching about them and praying with and for people to receive them.

I also found myself praying for and with people for all sorts of blessings and have seen the Lord answering our prayers in beautiful ways.

---

1   See Chapter 33.
2   See Chapter 34.

In writing this book, I want to bear witness to what I have seen and heard the Risen Lord doing in my life and the lives of people to whom I ministered.

I also want to give a platform for others who I know to share their testimonies. Many of these have already shared their testimony publicly. However, I hope that this book gives them a wider audience so they could reach and encourage many more in their faith.

After all, the charge that the Lord gave his disciples was "You will receive power when the Holy Spirit has come upon you, and you will be my witnesses", (Acts 1:8).

The charge fixed on us is to witness in the power of the Holy Spirit. The spreading of God's reign occurs as we bear witness.

As I chose the testimonies to share I found that both others and I use a language that may be strange and foreign for many people in our day. Not only non-Christians but also Christians may be unfamiliar with some of the words and expressions used, such as 'baptism in the Holy Spirit', 'charismatic gifts', 'resting in the Spirit', the 'gift of tongues', and so on. Hence, I decided to explain them briefly in Part Two and Part Three.

This book is neither about me nor others who share their stories but about the Risen Lord, about Jesus, our Healer. He continues his mission in our midst through his Body, the Church, and the power of the Holy Spirit. To say, 'Jesus our Healer' is another way of saying 'Jesus our Saviour'.

I hope to encourage and perhaps challenge many to open themselves more and more to the work of the Holy Spirit, so that Jesus would bring healing and salvation in their lives. This will empower them to bear witness to Him.

Some may ask that if this book is about healing why would I share testimonies about the grace of baptism in the Holy Spirit and the charismatic gifts? I believe that through the grace of baptism in the Holy Spirit, the Lord heals our sceptical minds and takes us to new horizons in our faith.

In most cases, I have used the names of the people whose stories I am telling. Where I have used other names, I will indicate this by adding: (Not his/her real name).

"The Lord has done great things for us, and we are filled with joy!" (Psalm 126:3).

1

How I experienced baptism in the Holy Spirit

"I baptise you with water for repentance. But after me comes one who is more powerful than I, whose sandals I am not worthy to carry. He will baptise you with the Holy Spirit and fire," (Matthew 3:11).

After attending a few charismatic prayer meetings back in 1972, a friend invited me to go on a weekend retreat at Thornleigh, New South Wales.

There were about 15 to 20 of us, including a priest. During the retreat, a couple of people shared about an experience they had had earlier. They referred to it as 'baptism in the Holy Spirit'. The term was unfamiliar to me. I soon discovered that 'being baptised in the Holy Spirit' was a biblical term. They shared that during their experience and after it they received charismatic gifts such as the gifts of tongues and prophecy.

Even though I was raised a Catholic and was active in the Young Christian Students Society (YCS) in Jerusalem where I was born, I was not familiar with the charismatic gifts. I must say I did not even know they existed. But here they are. We read about them in the first letter of St Paul to the Corinthians, chapters 12 to 14.

1 Corinthians 12:7-11 says:

Now to each one the manifestation of the Spirit is given for the common good. To one there is given through the Spirit a message of wisdom, to another a message of knowledge by means of the same Spirit, to another faith by the same Spirit, to another gifts of healing by that one Spirit, to another miraculous powers, to another prophecy, to another distinguishing between spirits, to another speaking in different kinds of tongues, and to still another the interpretation of tongues. All these are the work of one and the same Spirit, and he distributes them to each one, just as he determines.

Also, in the 'Decree on the Apostolate of the Laity' (*Apostolicam Actuositatem* in Latin), point 3, paragraph 3, we read:

The Holy Spirit sanctifies the People of God through the ministry and the sacraments. However, for the exercise of the apostolate he gives the faithful special gifts besides (cf. 1 Corinthians 12:7), "allotting them to each one as he wills" (1 Corinthians 12:11), so that each and all, putting at the service of others the grace received may be "as good stewards of God's varied gifts," (1 Peter 4:10), for the building up of the whole body in charity (cf. Ephesians 4:16). From the reception of these charisms, even the most ordinary ones, there arises for each of the faithful the right and duty of exercising them in the Church and in the world for the good of men and the development of the Church, of exercising them in the freedom of the Holy Spirit who "breathes where he wills" (John 3:8), and at the same time in communion with his brothers in Christ, and with his pastors especially.

I could not understand why I would need to be 'baptised in the Holy Spirit' since I was already baptised and in the Sacrament of Baptism I received the Holy Spirit. During the retreat, the leaders explained that we needed to "surrender" our lives to the Holy Spirit by renewing our baptismal vows and asking the Lord to baptise us with the Holy Spirit. It was not whether we possessed the Holy Spirit, but whether we were prepared to allow Him to "possess" us.

On Saturday night there was a prayer meeting. We sat in a circle singing hymns of praise and worship. The leader encouraged us to pray spontaneously; only a few did. Then we were invited to come forward to have a team pray with us if we wished to be baptised in the Holy Spirit. We all froze. When I saw that no one was coming forward, I decided to step forward, and they prayed with me. I explained that my stepping forward was to bear witness that I believed I had already received the Holy Spirit. They told me that it was fine.

I sat in the middle of the circle, and everybody gathered around me. The leaders and some of the participants gently placed their hands on my shoulder or "laid hands" on me as it was described to me. They explained that it was a sign of their unity and solidarity with me. I must admit that by then I was nervous and needed support. Then the leader led me in renewing my baptismal vows. Our conversation went like this:

Leader: "Do you reject Satan and all wrongdoing?"

Costandi: "Yes".

Leader: "Do you believe that Jesus died on the cross so that your sins would be forgiven and that he rose so that you may have life to the full?"

Costandi: "Yes".

Leader: "Will you accept Jesus as your Lord?"

Costandi: "Yes".

Leader: "Would you like Jesus to baptise you with the Holy Spirit?"

Costandi: "Yes".

The leader thanked God for the faith he had given me and prayed that He may fill me with the Holy Spirit. A few people joined in prayer; some prayed in tongues[1]. The leader asked me to praise the Lord aloud. I did not know how to do that. I repeated, "Praise God, praise God, praise you, God". I was becoming tense. The leader encouraged me to relax, so I took a deep breath and relaxed. Then I was told that the Lord wished to give me a gift. The leader asked me "Would you like to receive a gift from the Lord?" How could anyone say no to that? I answered, "Yes, if He wants to give me a gift, I will take it". Then the leader said "The Lord wishes to give you the gift of tongues". "Oh no, not that!" I thought. The leader encouraged me to continue praising God, not in English or any other language that I could speak, but to open my mouth and make a noise unto the Lord. So, I opened my mouth and made a noise, "aaa". I felt stupid, I felt humbled and at the same time overwhelmed with love. I felt God was so close and so real. I was filled with joy. I was laughing and crying at the same time. In my mind, I was thinking, "I am not worthy, I am not worthy". My joy intensified, and I found myself praising God with all my heart. Words that I did not understand were coming from my mouth like a machine gun. I did not want to stop praising God. This went for quite a few minutes; I don't know how long.

I was encouraged to move along so that they could pray with someone else. The next person was Sandra. I wanted to join everyone in praying for her. I wanted her to experience what I experienced. As I joined everyone else in prayer, I found myself praying in tongues again. It was awesome.

---

1   See Chapter 37.

This experience changed me! Here's how:

Before I received baptism in the Holy Spirit, I had low self-esteem. After receiving it, I knew God's love for me, and I started to blossom. Love changed me and I grew in confidence.

Before it, I was a slave to sin. After it, the pull of sin was less, and I discovered the power of the Holy Spirit, enabling me to say "no" to sin. I broke away from a habitual sin that had enslaved me for years.

Before it, I was always serious and self-occupied. After it, I was more relaxed and often smiling and more outgoing.

Before it, I liked reading the Bible when I got around to doing so. After it, I wanted to read the Bible whenever I had free time. I could relate to what I read; it made sense.

Before it, I hardly prayed. I attended Mass, but that's about it. After it, I wanted to pray all the time, and I could pray spontaneously. I experienced God speaking to me, teaching and guiding me. I also enjoyed prayer meetings and singing songs of praise. The hymn 'God is dwelling in my heart' became my favourite hymn:

God is dwelling in my heart; he and I are one.
All the joy he gives to me through Jesus Christ his Son.
And with Jesus in my heart, what have I to fear?
For he is the Son of God, in my heart he is near.

Before it, I knew about God. After it, I discovered a personal relationship with Jesus.

Before it, I performed religious observances. After it, I discovered a spiritual life.

Before it, I wanted to convince others about our faith. After it, I just wanted to bear witness about my experience with Jesus and pray with others to have a similar relationship with Him.

Before it, I felt powerless. After it, I discovered the power of the Holy Spirit is for us today as it was with the apostles in the New Testament. The power I received in my Baptism and Confirmation have become alive and active.

Before it, I did not feel I had much to offer others who needed healing. After it, I experienced the Lord's healing touch and found that I could pray with others, and the Lord healed many.

Before it, I always wanted to be part of a community. After it, I wanted not only to be part of a Catholic Christian Charismatic Covenant Community, but I received a call with others to build a Catholic Charismatic Covenant Community.

Before it, I had no direction, no mission. After it, united with Jesus and one with Him, I can say, "The Spirit of the Lord is on me because he has anointed me to preach good news to the poor. He has sent me to proclaim freedom for the prisoners and recovery of sight for the blind, to release the oppressed," (Luke 4:18).

Praise His Holy Name: Jesus!

2

Jesus healed me in many, many ways

"Bless the Lord, O my soul, and do not forget all his benefits who forgives all your iniquity, who heals all your diseases, who redeems your life from the pit, who crowns you with steadfast love and mercy, who satisfies you with good as long as you live so that your youth is renewed like the eagle's," (Psalm 103:2-5).

I met Sue (not her real name) at a young adults youth outreach of the Disciples of Jesus Covenant Community (DOJCC)[1]. Shortly after her first meeting, we were running 'Life in the Spirit', a series of seminars introducing people to the experience of the grace of baptism in the Holy Spirit.

After her experience of baptism in the Holy Spirit, I noticed a change in her. She was friendlier and seemed to be more part of the group.

---

1 See Chapter 42.

She attended a Youth Summer School of Evangelisation[2] which was run by the DOJCC. During the School, she came to see me with one of her friends. She was visibly upset and crying. When I asked her what was going on, she said she wanted us to pray with her seeking discernment. Instead of experiencing peace and joy, she felt she was feeling hurt and confused.

I met with Sue and explained that at times when we seek the Lord, He brings to mind hurts that we have experienced in the past because He desires to heal them. It's like when a goldsmith, who after melting the gold filings in a pot, stirs the molten metal so that all the impurities rise to the surface. Then the impurities are skimmed away, leaving behind the pure gold.

I asked Sue to tell me about her hurts. She related that someone close to her commented negatively at her appearance. She took it to heart as it was not the first time that kids made negative comments about her. She hated her body and wanted to change it by dieting; this led to her developing an eating disorder and seriously damaging her digestive system.

I explained to Sue that unforgiveness could be a real obstacle to receiving God's healing love. It's like when the sun is shining but clouds can come in the way. Therefore, it was important for her to decide to forgive all those who had hurt her.

I explained that forgiveness is not a feeling or an emotion but a decision that we make with our will, regardless of our feelings. We forgive because it is the right thing to do. Jesus forgave His enemies, even from the Cross, "Forgive them, Father, for they do not know what they are doing," (Luke 23:34).

---

2   See Chapter 43.

I prayed with Sue for the Father to give her the grace and the power to forgive. Then I led her into a prayer where she pronounced forgiveness to those people by name. When we forgive, we are healed and set ourselves free.

Following that, I led Sue in a prayer of repentance, asking the Lord's forgiveness for judging those people that hurt her and for abusing her body, which is a temple of the Holy Spirit (1 Corinthians 6:19). She did so willingly. It was then that I prayed over her for physical healing.

Sue gave the following sharing at Summer School[3] the following year:

"Hey, everybody, this was my experience from Summer School last year. I was brought up in a strict Catholic family, but when I turned 15, I started to fall away from the Church, and I fell away so much that I became so sick. I developed an eating disorder and depression. I stopped believing that Jesus cared about me at all. I thought, if He did care He wouldn't let me be feeling like this; so, if He doesn't care about me, then why should I care about Him? And I only went to Mass because I was dragged there by my parents, and I would doze through the homilies and would not take in anything whatsoever. My parents got desperate because I was attending an adolescent clinic at a hospital; it wasn't doing anything for me.

The parish priest told my parents about a young adults group. At first I flatly refused to go. I thought these people were freaks that wailed and thought that they were speaking a different language, and I just had no respect whatsoever for them.

Eventually, I went. At the time the youth group was running Life in the Spirit seminars. With some convincing, on the night of baptism of the Spirit, I went up to get prayed over. Praise God; I did experience the Holy Spirit coming

---

3   See Chapter 43.

through me in a way I have never felt before. I truly, truly felt God's love for me. I felt that He didn't want me to do what I was doing to my body. I saw myself as I indeed was, and how thin I truly was, and that was the night I decided to take my treatment seriously and change."

Experiencing God's love was Sue's first healing. Her other healing was that her eyes were opened, and she saw for herself how thin she was.

Sue went on to say:

"I did recover, praise God, but because of the abuses I had put my body through, I had damaged my digestive system. I couldn't eat without feeling extremely sick. I didn't feel hunger and fullness. I had really, really bad cramps that were so bad that I would just be lying on the couch in pain and unable to function. It reached a height before Summer School last year, and I did go and see a doctor. She put me on medication, but it didn't do anything for me, so she doubled the dosage. It still didn't do anything for me. By then it was too late, we had to leave for Summer School, so I thought, 'Well, I'm just going to have to live with it because I brought this on myself so I have to tough it out and see my doctor when I return home'.

I went up to be prayed over during the Summer School, and for some reason, it didn't occur to me to pray for healing at that stage. I didn't know much about it, but I went up and I asked for discernment in what I needed to do to be happy. Instead of feeling peace or happiness, I was overwhelmed by sadness and emotions I hadn't experienced again since my recovery a year ago. I didn't know what was going on; it freaked me out.

I went and saw Cosi with a friend. He told me that sometimes we think we have come past something, but we still have underlying issues. So that we can deal with them, God brings those issues to the surface and then skims them off the top. Cosi offered to do a prayer session with me for the healing of memories and the physical effects of the eating disorder. We did that the next day. As Cosi was praying for healing of the bad memories and the nightmares and unforgiveness I had towards other people, it started to go away. Again, I felt the Holy Spirit going through me, and I felt incredible peace. I started crying, and there were a lot of tissues involved. It was emotional, but it was awesome. And about halfway through, Cosi also started praying for healing from the physical effects to my digestive system, which that week had been bad. I was feeling sick.

He was praying and praying, and I was praying and crying, and suddenly, I felt this jolt here. I felt this warmth go from here to here (Sue pointed from her neck to her abdomen) through my body, and I started crying because it startled me, and I said to Cosi, 'What did you do? What did you do?' and he said, 'I didn't do anything, I was just praying', and we kept praying.

It hit me about a week later that everything was gone; all the cramps, all the pain, and I felt hungry. When you're sick with that disease, your brain stops registering feelings of hunger and fullness; you eat because you know that it is time you're supposed to eat. I felt hunger, fullness, no more cramps, all without medication. Jesus healed me in many, many ways.

I guess if it wasn't for the Summer School and learning about the gift of healing there, I may not have had that experience. The beautiful people that were around me were very supportive, without knowing that there was even anything wrong with me. Still, they were so lovely and supportive, and you could see the Spirit of God moving in them, and it was such a fantastic experience."

3

How I was set free from the addiction to smoking cigarettes

"'All things are lawful for me', but not all things are helpful. 'All things are lawful for me', but I will not be enslaved by anything," (1 Corinthians 6:12).

This is me, Costandi, sharing my own testimony. My addiction to cigarettes began on a trip from Jerusalem to Bethlehem. There were three of us in the car: Fr Michel (Michael) Sabbah, Victor, a friend, and me. When we were approaching an Israeli checkpoint, my hand reached to my shirt pocket for my ID card. It was not there.

"Turn right, turn right!" I shouted to Fr Michel who was driving. He turned into the street just before the checkpoint. We could not proceed without the ID card. We had to go back to Jerusalem to get it!

We were on our way to a leaders meeting of the Young Christian Students (YCS). We were running on time until then; now we were going to be at least 30 minutes late. In a moment of frustration, I asked my friend for a cigarette.

That was the first of many. It became a habit and an addiction.

After being baptised in the Holy Spirit, I continued to smoke. One day after a prayer meeting at River of Life Community in Newtown, NSW, Anne, a friend, asked me with disgust and pain on her face: "Cosi, why do you smoke? You are doing well, and everything is going well for you, why do you smoke?" Surprised, I said, "I like it", and shrugged it off.

But it got me thinking. Why do I smoke?

I was given many reasons by others why I shouldn't smoke: to save money, it was bad for my health, and so on. Nothing was convincing enough, or perhaps I did not want to be convinced. Perhaps I was afraid that I might not be able to stop smoking?

By then, I was smoking one to one-and-a-half packets a day. I smoked all the time. I smoked before breakfast. I smoked after breakfast. I smoked before I got on the train. I smoked when I got off the train before I started work. I smoked at morning tea. I smoked at the beginning of the lunch break. I smoked just before I returned to work. I smoked in the afternoon break. I smoked as I walked out of work. I smoked just before I got on the train and when I got off the train and so on.

I smoked when I got upset. I smoked when I was happy. I smoked when I was down on myself, and when I congratulated myself. Smoking had something to do with my emotions. I did not know how to handle them.

Someone said to me, "Costandi, your body is the temple of the Holy Spirit (1 Corinthians 6:19). Have you thought of that?" That really got me thinking.

One day I came across 1 Corinthians 6:12:

"'All things are lawful for me', but not all things are helpful. 'All things are lawful for me', but I will not be enslaved by anything."

Here I was teaching people that Jesus came and died for us to set us free, He rose that we may have a life to the full, yet I am a slave to smoking!

So I decided to stop smoking. I experienced headaches, tears, lack of concentration; I became irritable and a pain to those who were around me. This state lasted almost three weeks, but then I was back smoking!

I can not!

At the River of Life Community gatherings, I regularly gave short talks to newcomers about Jesus setting us free and baptism in the Holy Spirit.

Yet I was a slave to cigarettes.

I can't give up smoking. I need help!

At the end of one of our prayer meetings, we invited people to come forward for prayer ministry. People would come and ask for a blessing, a healing or a gift from the Lord.

So, I decided to ask for prayer to be set free from addiction to cigarettes. People gathered around and laid hands on me, and they prayed to Jesus to free me from addiction.

Jeff was leading the prayer. He prayed: "Lord take away from our brother even the desire to smoke". I responded enthusiastically with "Amen!"

Jeff asked me to surrender my packet of cigarettes. I gave it to him. Then he asked for my lighter as well. I surrendered that too. When Jeff took my packet of cigarettes and lighter from me, I felt relief. I went home with no cigarettes. I did not smoke before I went to bed.

The following morning, I reached for the cigarettes. 'Ah yes, I gave up smoking last night. The Lord has set me free'.

No headaches, no tears, no lack of concentration. Instead I experienced joy and a sense of freedom. This freedom became my treasure. "If the son of man sets you free you will be free indeed," (John 8:36). Praise the Lord; I am free from addiction to cigarettes.

Have I been tempted to smoke since? Sure. With God's grace, I have been free for decades now!

Reflecting on this experience, I learnt that one should:

Firstly, recognise that he or she has a problem.

Secondly, be humble and admit he or she needs to change and then make the decision to change.

Thirdly, discover "I can't".

Fourthly, call on the Lord. "Yes, Lord, you can. Lord, I need your help."

Those who call on the Lord will be saved!

"And everyone who calls on the name of the Lord will be saved," (Acts 2:21).

The story of Paul from Newcastle

Once when I was giving a talk about the basic Gospel message, I used my experience of being set free from my addiction to smoking to illustrate the point. I explained that we know we can't save ourselves and we need to turn to Jesus who loves us and has the power to save and heal. During the break, a well-built young man in his late twenties from the Newcastle area came to chat with me. It was a hot day, but he was wearing a long-sleeved top. He explained that his body was covered with tattoos. He was putting up with the heat because he did not want to give a bad example to the young people at the Summer School. He shared with me that he has been on drugs and all sort of things, and he managed to give up most of these addictions but could not give up smoking. He asked me to pray with him. We prayed and asked the Lord, who died on the Cross to save us, to set him free from that slavery and to heal him emotionally as well.

Four months later, I received an Easter card from him. He thanked me and said he had given up smoking since we prayed together. He wrote that that particular Easter was a special one for him and that he can now say he has experienced the power of the Resurrection. He shared that since giving up smoking he had saved enough money to go on a pilgrimage to Medjugorje, which he was very much looking forward to.

4

He just keeps on surprising me

"Dear friends, let us love one another, for love comes from God. Everyone who loves has been born of God and knows God," (1 John 4:7).

I received this email from a young lady who shared with me how God had worked in her life:

Hi Cosi,

Hope you remember who I am, I know you know a LOT of people.

I think the last time I saw you was in Canberra for vows with the MGL Sisters[1]... when Amanda and I had breakfast with you guys at McDonald's.

Anyway, Cosi, I just wanted to write a quick email to let you know that things have been really different

---
1   *See Chapter 43.*

for me since Summer School. I want to thank you from the bottom of my heart for your faithfulness and love. You give of yourself tirelessly, and during an especially busy week at Summer School. You still made time to pray with me and not just half-heartedly, but as though I was the only person there!

I thank God for the gifts He has given to you – He blesses us through you! God has especially blessed me as I received healing when you prayed over me (physically and emotionally). I had big problems with my ovaries, and it seems to be a lot better, even though I stopped all treatment.

Emotionally, I can hardly explain the joy in my heart. Truly, Cosi, you prayed that I would feel loved and learn to love myself. And Jesus just keeps on surprising me! I am beginning to feel whole again! Praise God!

You're in my prayers and hope to see you 'around' sometime soon.

God Bless, Alissa.

God is love. Love heals body, soul and spirit! He gives real joy. When love heals, He enables you to love yourself. When you love yourself, you can love others too. When you live in love, you are born of God. What a privilege it is to be a channel of His Love! What joy it is!

"The thing the Church needs most today is the ability to heal wounds and to warm the hearts of the faithful; it needs nearness, proximity. I see the Church as a field hospital after battle," (Pope Francis).

"May the God of peace himself sanctify you entirely; and may your spirit and soul and body be kept sound and blameless at the coming of our Lord Jesus Christ," (1 Thessalonians 5:23).

5

Patience and trust as God came through in the end...

"Does a woman forget her baby at the breast, or fail to cherish the son of her womb? Yet even if these forget, I will never forget you," (Isaiah 49:15).

It was late at night when I received a phone call from Marita. "I think I met my future husband," she said. "I want you to be one of the first people to know," she went on to say. Marita was so happy.

I was delighted with the news and felt honoured. Marita asked me to pray for guidance because this is the woman she is, a woman of faith who always wants to do God's will.

Marita shared:

"While I had come to a deep relationship with God and wanted to give my life to him, I also felt called to be a wife and mother. But it took a long time to meet the right man, and many times I despaired that it would ever happen. I prayed and prayed that God would answer my cry. 'Where is your faith?' (Luke 8:25)."

I have had the privilege to minister to many single, beautiful women of God who were looking for husbands. I was always struck by the many who placed their relationship with the Lord above their desire for a husband. They refused to compromise their faith values.

The deepest root of Christian womanhood is hope in God. Marita continued:

"Then, in 2002, I was invited by a friend to her housewarming party. It was a really fun night. There was also a lovely man there, a close friend. He was very attentive to me that night. I went to sleep with a smile on my face thinking about him.

A few weeks later we met by coincidence (or 'God-incidence') at St Patrick's, Church Hill – in inner Sydney – at Mass one Sunday afternoon. It was not my usual Mass, but I ended up there after a family function earlier in the day. After Mass he invited me out to a game of rugby – I was pleased to accept.

We continued to meet, got to know one another, and enjoyed each other's company. I described him in my prayer journal as 'sweet, gentle and kind'."

Marita's courtship lasted for 18 months, after which she became engaged, and in 2005 she was married.

Marita was looking forward to having children.

She said: "I thought that once we were married, we would be quickly and easily blessed with babies. In our first year of marriage we lost our first baby, at six weeks gestation. I felt like a failure as a woman!"

Marita felt devastated.

She continued: "I turned to Cosi for prayer, both for healing and for another baby."

Ministering to Marita, I could sense her deep pain and grief. I felt the Lord would bless her with a child again.

"We also sought out a Catholic doctor who could assist us with fertility care which is in accordance with Church teaching," Marita recalled.

Seeking medical help is not a sign of lack of faith. Faith does not cancel common sense, and common sense is not contrary to faith. The word of God instructs us:

"Honour physicians for their services, for the Lord created them; for their gift of healing comes from the Most High... My child, when you are ill, do not delay, but pray to the Lord, and he will heal you," (Ecclesiasticus 39:1-2, 9).

In 2009, the Lord blessed Marita and her husband with a beautiful, heathy baby girl whom they named Elizabeth. They rejoiced and praised God!

However, pain and grief struck again.

"Two more pregnancies ended in tears, one at eight weeks and the other at 12 weeks. I knew that the souls of our angels went right to heaven, but where was God in answering our prayers? Lots of trust was required, and so many times I failed to trust God and his love for me and gave in to despair," Marita recalled.

The God of surprises heard their cry and visited them again.

Marita went on to say: "Life continued, and we were about to renovate a home for our family of three to move into. The God of surprises had other ideas, and later that year, 2014, we were delighted to welcome another daughter. Elizabeth had been asking Jesus to send her a little sister, and here was Grace."

And isn't it an appropriate name?

"It has been quite a journey for our family, with healing from loss and hurt and two miracle babies. God's love is everlasting," declared Marita.

"Take delight in the Lord, and He will give you the desires of your heart. Commit your way to the Lord, trust in Him, and He will act," (Psalm 37:4, 5).

6

Barbara found her father

"He sent His word and healed them!" (Psalm 107:20).

Pain, more pain, a Word of Knowledge, the Father's love, and healing!

Shortly after my beloved wife Barbara and I met, we both recognised that the Lord meant us to be with each other. How we met is another story for another time! The following is Barbara's story.

Barbara told me that her father left her and her mum when she was two years old. Barbara and her mother suffered much emotional and financial hardship because of his decision. Barbara felt anger and resentment towards her father, and also pain, grief and rejection all her life.

As she grew up her mother would say to her, "Well, you know, it would be good if you felt like it, you could try and find your father". But she didn't do anything about it.

It wasn't until Barbara started to get more into her faith that she found great difficulty in wanting to know and understand God the Father, as she had not experienced an earthly father. She remembered her mother's suggestion to search for her father and contacted the Salvation Army's Missing Persons Bureau, who started the search.

While Barbara was waiting for news, she was struggling in her mind. She shared her thoughts with me, "Wow! What if I could find him and then I could ask him all the things I'd always wanted to ask, and I'd have a real dad in my life".

But then she was haunted with the thoughts, 'What if he has already died? What if I never find him?' and she feared the grief of losing him a second time.

Twelve months later, it turned out that her father was dead. In fact, the time when she initiated the search was around the time of his death.

"It was like someone plunged a serrated knife into my heart, and was turning it backward and forward, leaving me with a big hole in my heart." Barbara described her real heart-wrenching grief with me time and time again. No matter how I tried to comfort her, it was to no avail.

Barbara was stuck with this most dreadful, gut-wrenching feeling for many years.

One night, we went to our usual charismatic prayer meeting. Barbara recalls: "It was winter, and it was cold, it was dark. I wanted to go home, but I sat there barely enduring the cold."

During the meeting, someone gave a Word of Knowledge[1] saying, "God wants to heal someone here who has a deep pain".

---

1   See Chapter 38.

Barbara was sitting there not taking much notice, until she thought "Whoever you are, God is talking to you! Just claim that Word, and we can all go home or at least have a hot cup of coffee".

Minutes passed. After no one had claimed that Word, Barbara thought, 'Oh, okay. Well, that relates to me. Okay, God, if it's for me, yes, I claim the Word'. Barbara recalls: "I wasn't feeling particularly holy, religious, spiritual or anything that evening, and I completely forgot about it."

Barbara decided to receive that Word for herself and asked the prayer team to pray with her. During the prayer session, Barbara had to forgive her father and to thank God for being her real father.

Barbara continues:

"About one year later, something came up that reminded me of this experience. I realised that the terrible wrenching pain that I had carried for so long was gone! It just wasn't there anymore. I had the memory of everything happening, but all the pain, grief and anguish that went with it just wasn't there. I realised that God *was* talking to me. My Eternal Father was saying, 'I'll never leave you. I'll be with you always, and I don't want you to suffer that pain any more. I want to be your daddy'.

I am touched to my core to know that Almighty God wants to be my dad. I have a daddy who will always love me, and I can always depend on Him."

Barbara made the words of Psalm 73 her own:

"Father, 'I am continually with you;
you hold my right hand.
Father, you guide me with your counsel,
and afterwards, you will receive me to glory.
Whom have I in heaven but you?
And there is nothing on earth that I desire besides you.
My flesh and my heart may fail,

but God is the strength of my heart and my portion forever.
For me it is good to be near God;
I have made the Lord God my refuge,
that I may tell of all your works.'
PS - Your loving daughter, Babs."

The Holy Spirit gave a 'Word of Knowledge' to someone at the prayer meeting. A man stepped out in faith, shared the 'Word'. The 'Word' eventually attracted Barbara's attention. She thought the person referred to should respond. That person was her.

She accepted that Word as a promise for herself.

"The word of God is alive and active," (Hebrews 4:12).

The Word became a reality. The pain is gone. The memories are still there, but she is now free from the pain.

The Father's love heals. The Father, who is Love, heals.

"I will never forget you. I have carved you in the palms of my hands," (Isaiah 49:16).

7

Jesus continues to set the oppressed free

"For in my inner being I delight in God's law; but I see another law at work in me, waging war against the law of my mind and making me a prisoner of the law of sin at work within me. What a wretched man I am! Who will rescue me from this body that is subject to death? Thanks be to God, who delivers me through Jesus Christ our Lord!" (Romans 7:22-25).

In His love for us, God does not only forgive us our sins but also heals us and restores us so we can live life to the full as He intended for us from the beginning.

Overcoming impure thoughts

I am grateful to 'Peter' (not his real name), for sharing his story of overcoming impure memories. I am sure this will be an encouragement to many who have similar struggles:

"Hi Costandi,

I hope you are well. I was praying the other day and was reminded that I'd never told you what happened to me after you prayed with me at Summer School last year.

Leading up to Summer School, I had been troubled frequently with impure memories, which hurt me a lot whenever they popped into my head. When you prayed with me to be free from them, I was struggling to believe that God would take them away with a prayer like this (I'm often too much of a sceptic!). I certainly didn't think that it would happen quickly, but I chose to be open to His work.

I realised a couple of days later, to my surprise and joy, the pain had been taken out of the memories. I could quickly push them aside without being troubled by them. These days I am not troubled by them at all.

This was important for me, especially leading up to marriage. A deep fear of mine was that what I had done previously would prevent me from properly honouring my fiancée.

So, I just wanted to say, thank you for allowing God to work through you and for sharing His grace with others.

God Bless, Peter."

Overcoming 'bad thoughts'

I know a priest who loves the Lord and His people. He is a humble man. It was a joy to pray with him. I was sure the Lord would set him free. In my prayer, I thanked God for the gift this man of God is for many people. Then I asked him to command the evil spirit that was harassing him to 'begone' in the name of Jesus. I joined him in that command. There were no visible signs of any change. However, he noticed a difference, and this is his testimony:

"I am a priest. Costandi prayed over me in March, 2012. I had 'bad thoughts' that I could not shake. For a few years these thoughts were often unrelenting and their intensity increasing. After he prayed for a few minutes the thoughts disappeared. That was just over a month ago."

The Lord taught us to pray, "Lead us not into temptation". He also added, "But deliver us from the evil one". At Mass we also pray, "Deliver us, Lord, from every evil and grant us peace in our days".

As sons and daughters of God we share in the anointing of Christ – Priest, Prophet and King – and hence we have the authority to command, in the name of Jesus, the evil spirits that are harassing us or obsessing us, to leave us.

Here I'm not talking about evil possession and exorcism. When evil possession is discerned, the Church teaches us that we need to seek prayer of Exorcism by priests specially appointed by the Church for that purpose.

"Again, truly I tell you, if two of you agree on earth about anything you ask, it will be done for you by my Father in heaven. For where two or three are gathered in my name, I am there among them," (Matthew 18:19-20).

When we request prayer, we are humbling ourselves and exercising our faith in God.

"The devil is like a mad dog tied by a chain. Beyond the length of the chain he cannot catch hold of anyone. And you, therefore, keep your distance. If you get too close you will be caught. Remember, the devil has only one door with which to enter our soul: our will. There are no secret or hidden doors. No sin is a true sin if we have not wilfully consented," (Saint Padre Pio of Pietrelcina).

8

Untie that donkey, for I have use for it

"The Spirit of the Lord is upon me, because he has anointed me to bring good news to the poor. He has sent me to proclaim release to the captives and recovery of sight to the blind, to let the oppressed go free, to proclaim the year of the Lord's favour," (Luke 4:18-19).

Christine, a member of our community, forwarded this message to Barbara and I:

"Hello. I just tried calling from Rockingham, Western Australia. My name is Tarena-Ann. My mum and dad used to take me to gatherings led by Costandi and Barbara Bastoli over 25 years ago. I will never forget the great love shown. They have both been in my heart lately and I am trying to contact them. If you could pass this message on to them, I would really appreciate it, as it was on this date, 17 January, many years ago, that I received great healing. Praise be the name of Jesus."

When I saw it, my heart leapt with joy! I remembered Tarena-Ann very well. I often shared what the Lord had done for her, mainly when ministering to young women who suffered from a similar condition. So I phoned her. When she answered, I asked, "Is this Princess Tarena?" A burst of joy came from the other end of the line, "Oh Costandi, it is so wonderful to hear your voice". Then I tried to catch up on 25 years of her life since Barbara and I ministered God's love to her.

Barbara and I were on a prayer team praying for the sick at a charismatic Healing Mass organised by our community. I saw a couple with their young daughter, who was about 15 years old, sitting in the second row. They came to us for prayer. I noticed the daughter could hardly walk and she needed her parents to assist her.

Tarena seemed anorexic. Her parents explained that she was refusing to eat and hadn't eaten for a while. She had received medical and psychological help but to no avail. Her parents were delighted that she agreed to come to the Healing Mass. They were hopeful that the Lord would heal her.

When I saw Tarena, she seemed as if she was walking 'in the shadow of death'. As we were ministering to her, I encouraged and assisted her to decide to choose life, which she verbalised in a prayer, repeating the words after me.

She asked, "Is it okay to eat?" I shared with her how St Francis of Assisi referred to his body as 'Brother Donkey' and that a donkey once carried Jesus in his triumphant entry into Jerusalem. We need to look after our 'donkey'.

I also encouraged and assisted her in receiving the Lord's forgiveness for not eating and thus neglecting to care for her body which is the temple of the Holy Spirit.

In our telephone conversation, Tarena started to share with me her recollections of the time she received the healing from the Lord. I asked her to write it down and send it to me. She wrote:

"Costandi,

I thank my mum and dad for taking me to church every Sunday while growing up. Although I never quite understood much, I knew Jesus would always be with me and help me.

I developed anorexia nervosa at age 12. I remember lying in bed, crying to Jesus that 'I would like to eat again, without any guilt'.

The next day, mum and dad showed me a flyer for a healing service the Disciples of Jesus community were organising. I knew I had to go, and I knew Jesus was the only one who could heal me and take away the shame and guilt from being indecently assaulted at age four."

At the time, Tarena did not share details of her abuse.

Tarena continued:

"After being prayed over, a shift occurred within me. I went home and asked for a cup of tea and fruit cake. The guilt had gone!"

In her letter, Tarena wrote to me:

"I remember that you told me I am a daughter of the King, and you asked me what that makes me. I answered a princess! I have shared this truth with so many young girls and their eyes light up.

Another thing I remember is that you told me I was a donkey.

Two Christmases ago, I watched an animation of the Nativity called 'The Star'. It was the story of a donkey held in captivity as a mill donkey. In the end, this little donkey carried Mary and Joseph until the birth of Jesus. I couldn't stop crying as your words many years ago spoke through this movie."

Tarena continued:

"Even today, the healing continues. Unfortunately, on a few more occasions, my innocence was stolen from me, which led me to be always on the go, not having to deal with traumatic flashbacks. Being a cleaner for 20 years was a great way of running away and hiding.

This lifestyle has led to bone-on-bone double-hip arthritis at age 40 – so now no more cleaning!

Yet deep within I am grateful that all this has happened, as I now realise I should have run to Jesus, not away from Him.

It is because of Jesus that I can walk! "In Him, I live and move and have my being," (Acts 17:28). If it was not for Him, I should be in a wheelchair.

My condition led me to share the good news with those who suffer from addictions, drugs, alcohol, and anyone who is trying to escape from past traumatic events.

I am learning now that it is okay to have emotions and feelings... it is what we do with them, and the best thing ever is to run to Jesus, who takes all the pain away.

You both genuinely have been anointed to bring the good news, set the captives free and restore sight (physical and spiritual) to the blind (Luke 4:18)."

Tarena also wrote:

"Costandi and Barbara, I will always remember your words about being a donkey. The little donkey who carries our Lord Jesus. You both also carry our Lord Jesus wherever you go, bringing gentle words of love, mercy, compassion and healing. Many will give praise to our Saviour, and He will heal many of addiction and all things that bind them, as Jesus gave the command 'untie that donkey, for I have use for it' (Mark 11:2-3).

May God bless you and your powerful ministry.

Love, Tarena."

I also remembered that three weeks after praying with Tarena, her father, Brian, phoned to thank Barbara and I. He wanted us to know that Tarena was well on her way to recovery. She was regularly eating and had put on weight. He also said that the first change they had seen in her was on the way home from ministry; she smiled and seemed happy for the first time in years.

Often people ask if healing received through prayer lasts or is it only psychological and temporary. Here is Tarena, 25 years later, still rejoicing in her healing and remembering the actual date of her encounter with Jesus. She has gone to great lengths to find us and share her joy.

Let us thank our Lord for saving Tarena from anorexia nervosa and that He may heal her from arthritis!

"To tell of the works of the Lord is to give praise," (Cassiodorus).

9

When a healing does not come immediately!

"Then Jesus told them a parable about their need to pray always and not to lose heart," (Luke 18:1).

In January, 2009 at Summer School, I prayed with Hannah for the Lord to heal her from eczema.

I saw Hannah a few months later, on Good Friday at the biannual Light to the Nations pilgrimage[1]. I was feeling tired and sad and a bit down as I reflected on the Passion of the Lord. Hannah came running to me saying, "Hi Cosi". I said, "Hey Hannah", and she quickly pulled up her sleeve. I thought she wanted me to pray over her again.

But she said, "Look Cosi, it's all gone". I was happily surprised. Wanting to know more, I said, "What happened after I prayed with you?" She told me that she went and spent some time with the Lord in front of the Blessed

---

[1] See Chapter 44.

Sacrament. The following week she went on holiday with her family. She noticed that her eczema was getting better, and after a while, she was healed completely.

Why was I surprised? I know that our Lord hears our prayers, but not always the way we expect Him to. In her innocence and sincere faith, Hannah expected Him to heal her instantly. That didn't happen. She continued to hope. How often we give up on God too soon!

When Hannah shared with me about the Lord healing her, it lifted my spirit that Good Friday.

Later I saw Jennie, Hannah's mother, and I asked how long Hannah had suffered with eczema. I also asked if she wouldn't mind writing down what happened so that with the right facts, I could use the story when teaching on God's healing love.

Jennie sent me the following:

"My daughter Hannah is 10 years old and has suffered from eczema, which is a skin condition, most of her life. As she has grown over the years, especially the last two years, it has become much worse. Eczema would appear behind her knees and elbows and at times would become so inflamed that she would be in pain from the soreness. It showed itself as a bright red rash which often made her feel self-conscious.

At Christmas last year Hannah was becoming more concerned about comments other kids were making regarding her eczema. I realised it was time to see a specialist - in the new year. In January, our family attended a Catholic youth week where young adults had the opportunity to listen to lectures on their Catholic faith and also to learn about the charismatic gifts. It was during this week that we had a night where people could go forward for prayer for any area in their lives.

During the night, Hannah approached me and asked if she could go up for prayer for her eczema. I encouraged her to go to Costandi as he is a close member of the family, and also, I was aware he has a strong gift of healing. Cosi prayed over her gently. Afterwards, she went to sit before the Blessed Sacrament to pray.

Over the rest of the week, I didn't think much more about Hannah's prayer experience, and we said our goodbyes from the wonderful week and headed off to Forster for a week's holiday with the family. It wasn't till midweek that Hannah told me to take a look at her eczema. To my surprise, the rash had faded to a light pink colour. A few weeks later it had disappeared entirely – never to be seen again.

Hannah has been free of eczema since the prayer that night. We are truly grateful to Jesus for His kindness in Hannah's healing but also how her faith has grown through this experience. Cosi, your 'Yes' to our Lord is a blessing in our lives."

I have asked Hannah to share her testimony several times in healing seminars that I conducted at Summer School. Here is a transcription of the testimony she gave four years later:

"When I was about 10 years old, I had severe eczema. I have suffered with it since I was born. It was all up my arms and behind my legs. It was a struggle as I was growing up because at school, I had friends who asked what was wrong with me, why my skin was in different colours, and I would always be uncomfortable. There would be days where I would wear a long-sleeved shirt to cover it. I was a little girl, so I was very insecure.

I knew about God because I had grown up in a Christian family. At Summer School, I heard that Cosi has a prayer ministry and that he prayed for healing. I thought 'Well, maybe I should ask him to pray with me'. I guess I was pretty nervous because only big people went to the prayer teams, but I was just over my eczema. I didn't want to have to deal with it any longer.

I thought, 'Well, God is good. He will heal me straight away. I will go into this prayer, and I will come out, and I will be completely healed'. So, I went for prayer, and I prayed to get healed from my eczema. It didn't heal miraculously like happens in some stories.

I was so young, and I didn't know that God could take His time to heal me. I didn't understand that God does everything in His time, that He has a plan for me. So, I was kind of 'Oh, that didn't work. I'll have to be insecure again'. But then after Summer School we went away to Forster and about a week or so later, not that it had disappeared yet, but it wasn't itching that much anymore! I noticed a bit of difference, but I didn't think about it so much. I was just kind of like, oh, it was probably not anything too special. But by about three weeks later or so, I had no eczema on my arms or behind my legs. The Lord healed me from what the doctors diagnosed me with as a baby. Now, I have not suffered from it since. I no longer have to use any treatment or anything. I used to have to visit doctors. I don't have to do that anymore. And, yes, the Lord saved me from eczema!"

Hannah finished her testimony, saying, "The Lord saved me from eczema". Yes, healing is salvation. Hannah now knows from experience something about salvation.

Hannah knew from her upbringing that God is good – all the time! Now from experience, she learned that God does things in His good timing.

His answer was not 'No' but 'Not yet!' It was gradual healing. In the process, she learned to persevere and never to lose hope.

Hannah gives thanks every time she bears witness to what the Lord has done for her. She is like that leper who was healed by Jesus and returned to give thanks.

Thank you, Hannah, for your witness and your faith and for sharing it with me and others.

"Amen, I say to you, whatever you ask in prayer, believe that you will receive, and it shall be given to you, says the Lord," (Mark 11:23-24).

10

From His fullness
Grace received grace!

"From his fullness we have all received grace upon grace. The law indeed was given through Moses; grace and truth came through Jesus Christ. No one has ever seen God. It is God the only Son, [who is close to the Father's heart], who has made him known,"
(John 1:14-18).

Grace came to Summer School.

Grace stated: "I didn't want to be here at all. I wanted to leave and go home."

But on Thursday night, something happened that changed her life.

Grace testified:

"On Thursday night, baptism in the Spirit night, I went up to a prayer team. I was one of the last people that went up for prayer. I went to Costandi and an MGL brother. I got up there, and I renewed my Baptismal promises, rejecting Satan and proclaiming Jesus as my leader for the rest of my life. As I was praying, I felt alone. I felt God had just left me completely. I went seeking life but felt nothing was happening, nothing going on at all."

She sounded very disappointed as she said that.

Grace went on to testify:

"Then Cosi said that God wanted to give me the gift of love, and instantly my heart just opened, and I began crying, which is so unusual for me, I never do that, I never do that in public. I was crying, crying and crying and quite soon after, I fell to the ground, resting in the Holy Spirit[1]. I was lying on the ground and God's love was pouring into my heart. I was so happy, I was smiling, and I began laughing ecstatically, I couldn't stop laughing. These fits of laughter took over the whole of my body, and at one point, I felt like someone was tickling me, the whole of my body was tickling. My toes curled, and I was just so happy.

I was so joyous because God loves me, I knew it, and I felt it. It's like both Jesus and I were laughing together. We were laughing about how anxious I get with my troubles, and how much I overthink things. Together we were just laughing because He is so much bigger than that. It was like a breeze along His ankles. He is so much bigger than my troubles. We were laughing together because I knew it for the first time in my life."

When Grace eventually got up, I invited her to join in praying with a brother who was waiting for the healing of his back. So she did.

The following is what happened.

Grace said, "I got up and had received the gift of healing, not just my healing, but the gift of praying for healing for other people as well. So together with Cosi, we

---

[1] *See Chapter 39.*

prayed over an MGL brother who had back pain. I watched as I was praying in tongues over this man. I watched his heels. One leg was one and a half centimetres longer than the other. I watched them as they came perfectly together. Then the same happened with his arms. One arm seemed longer than the other by about one centimetre. They came together perfectly. Then we were praying over his back and his neck and recalling Jesus' pain on the Cross as his head was dropping. Then the pain was gone, and he was healed of the pain that was troubling him."

This experience had an enormous impact on Grace.

She described her feelings: "I felt so light, and the glory of God was just shining through this moment, and I couldn't contain myself, it was so beautiful".

This experience drew her to the Lord in the Blessed Sacrament.

"I went over to the Blessed Sacrament, and I was adoring, adoring God and our Lord and swaying and dancing. I had never done that in public," Grace added.

Her joy was very obvious to all.

"One of my friends who was passing by, he came up to me and said, 'You look radiant'. He started giggling a little bit, and I started laughing again. It was a complete change in me. I don't think I could ever go back; I feel so loved and joyously loved by God; yes, thank you," Grace testified.

It was such a delight for me to see Grace's transformation, to see the Word of God coming into her life.

Grace will never forget this experience. She will no doubt remember it in good times and in hard times. The love of the Lord is constant. It never changes. It is true for every one of us when we feel it and when we don't.

11

From fear to faith

"(Jesus) said to them, 'It is I; do not be afraid,'"
(John 6:20).

In this story, we see an example of how the Holy Spirit works to set people free and heal them from fears. He gently increases our faith and trust in Him and grants us gifts to enable us to praise God with joy.

My experience of the 'sober inebriation of the Holy Spirit', by Simone Smith

"In early 2010 I received what is sometimes called the 'baptism' or 'outpouring' of the Holy Spirit. I had been a committed follower of Christ after a conversion experience in 2005 and receiving the Sacrament of Confirmation in 2006. Someone explained to me that to receive the outpouring of the Holy Spirit all you had to do was renew your baptismal vows and be open to receiving the same Holy Spirit you had received in the Sacraments of Baptism and Confirmation. I was happy to do so. Also, people had 'prayed over' me before. That is, people had prayed with and for me, and sometimes in tongues. However, I always had trouble understanding the gift of tongues[1]. I accepted that it was a gift of the Holy Spirit but wondered what the 'deal' was with this gift – why did the Lord give this language where the person was not aware of what they were saying? Also, from the outside, it seemed like a loss of the senses, a loss of control, whereby a person was taken over in a way that looked scary. Some of the reactions that people sometimes experienced after being prayed over frightened me - such as excessive crying or falling over backwards. These things also seemed like a loss of control of the body and the senses.

At the same time, I was frustrated with myself for being afraid. I knew by faith and experience that the Holy Spirit never forces us to do or receive anything and that He is always gentle. I was feeling quite anxious and conflicted, so amid all these fears while I was awaiting my turn for prayer, I took up the Rosary to invoke Mary's intercession, and this gave me a certain sense of peace.

When it came time for me to receive prayer, I was still afraid but also confident that God never forces His gifts upon us. And so the gifts and 'reactions' that I was scared of would not be forced upon me; I did not want the gift of tongues, and I knew the Lord would not give it to me because of this. As we began the prayer and I read out the renewal of my baptismal promises, I saw that the prayer specifically asked for the gift of tongues as well as other gifts. Being a person who tries never to say what I don't mean, I merely skipped over this invocation for the gift of tongues.

Either through habit or the direct inspiration of the Holy Spirit, the man who was praying over me almost

---

1   *See Chapter 37.*

immediately prayed for the gift of tongues. Although remaining silent, I inwardly said a firm 'no' to this gift. Nothing dramatic happened, of course, the prayer went on, yet I was feeling quite uneasy, thoughts went through my mind that this 'wouldn't work' and was a 'waste of time', and I even contemplated just running out of the room. However, I stuck it out and prayed inwardly that I might be able to let go of everything and surrender to the Lord. Those praying over me prayed for a 'breakthrough in the Spirit' and encouraged me to let go and surrender to the Lord. I tried to with all my heart. Suddenly, I was filled with a sense of peace and warmth, and before I quite knew what was happening, I was gently swaying, but surprisingly there was no fear. I felt that I had the choice to let go completely and I did, and I fell back and experienced God's love and peace. As I fell, I felt utterly safe and unafraid. As I lay there, I felt peace and love where there had been fear and insecurity. After this experience I felt real freedom from some past fears and wounds. I could start anew in my journey with the Lord. I was particularly strengthened for a new chapter in my life as I was about to move interstate for studies.

This experience was in January, 2010. A year-and-a-half passed by and I continued to have experiences with forms of charismatic prayer and to hear people praying in tongues. I began to wonder more about this gift, especially as I progressed in my prayer life and desired to pray with more silence and fewer words cluttering my thoughts during mental prayer. I began to see that perhaps the gift of tongues was another way of praying, that, like silent contemplation allowed the person to lift their heart to God in the act of pure loving prayer. One day after thinking a lot about this, I said to the Lord interiorly that should He wish to give me the gift of tongues, I was open to receiving it. Where before I had said a firm 'no' I now said 'yes'. Thinking that He may deliver straight away, I opened my mouth and tried to pray in tongues (I was by myself in a small chapel). Nothing happened, and I laughed at myself and went on with life as usual.

About a month or so later, the feast of Pentecost was approaching. On that day I was to have the first session teaching a teenage girl about the sacraments. So, in preparation for this, I prayed a novena to the Holy Spirit for His gifts.

The day of Pentecost came, and I had a beautiful session with the girl and went to Holy Mass with her. As I came back home, I was so full of joy over her openness and how well the teaching had gone. I knelt before the Lord in the tabernacle in a small chapel (I lived in a Catholic boarding house) and began to pray out loud thanking Him for the day, and before I knew it, I was praying out aloud in tongues. Just like that! It was as if the joy in my heart overflowed into my mouth, and I was given over to praising God and thanking Him. I began to sing in tongues. I experienced such freedom in praise and prayer. I believe that had I not been alone with the Lord, I would not have felt such freedom but may have been self-conscious. Although I felt 'taken over' in a sense, I also felt totally in control, my will and God's action were one.

I marvel at the fact that the Lord was so good and gracious to me, so gentle and accommodating that He would wait that long for me to say yes and to give me a gift which I had initially rejected. Since receiving the gift of tongues, I have found it is a great gift that allows me to pray when I have no words to pray with and to intercede for the needs of others from the heart. Also, receiving this gift has made me more open to accepting whatever God wants to give me as I know that it will be for my good and that there is nothing to fear.

The Fathers of the Church spoke of the 'sober inebriation' or 'intoxication' of the Holy Spirit – where one is overwhelmed by the power and presence of the Holy Spirit, yet without losing the faculty of reason, but rather having it filled with light. The Franciscan priest, Fr Raniero Cantalamessa OFM Cap, Preacher to the Pontifical Household, has written a book on precisely this theme. He notes that the sober intoxication of the Holy Spirit is an intoxication that brings purification from sin, renewal of heart and intuitive, experiential knowledge of God accompanied by joy. My own experience of the outpouring of the Holy Spirit brought me a renewal of heart, great peace of soul, and joy. My fears of losing control were completely put to rest as I experienced this 'sober intoxication' and the utter gentleness of God."

As Simone shared, receiving the gift of tongues opens a doorway to other blessings.

12

From scepticism to certainty

"The Spirit of Truth will bear witness to me, says the Lord," (John 15:26).

Kristin attended my lectures of the 'Life in the Holy Spirit' at the Disciples of Jesus Summer School of Evangelisation in Bathurst. It was a series of five lectures over five days, Monday to Friday. During the first lecture, Kristin seemed uninterested and somewhat sceptical.

Her attitude started to change gradually. Her experience on Thursday night was a definite turning point.

Giving her testimony, Kristin introduced herself, saying:

"Hi, my name is Kristin. I'm from Our Lady of the Rosary, Kellyville.

Disciples of Jesus Summer School of Evangelisation 2014 was my first charismatic experience ever. I was raised as a traditional Catholic. My sister made sure that I went to Summer School that year. At the beginning of the week, I was closed-minded to charismatic prayer, the gift of speaking in tongues and other charismatic gifts and that sort of thing. By Friday, all that had changed. During the School, I learnt a lot about the gifts and the importance of the Holy Spirit.

There are so many gifts of the Holy Spirit. God wants to give them to us if we have the grace to ask for them," Kristin asserted.

Kristin described what she had experienced on the night of her baptism in the Holy Spirit.

"Thursday night was the baptism in the Holy Spirit[1] night. The Mass was beautiful.

After the Mass, I thought 'All right, I will go and get prayed with straight away'. I felt I was ready. I made sure I asked for Cosi because Cosi was giving the lectures. So, I waited a while. As I was waiting, I listened to the praise and worship. The words of the hymn were really powerful and beautiful and got to me. I started crying. Then when I went up to be prayed over, I was a little bit nervous. I just listened to the praying around me in tongues. One of the ladies was singing, and it was beautiful.

Then I renewed my baptismal vows, and I asked God for the gift of wisdom. That is all that I asked for, but when I was saying the words, and people were praying over me, I felt a lot of emotion was happening. I continued to cry. Then Cosi asked me to start praising God. I repeated the words, 'I thank you, Jesus. I love you, Jesus. I praise you, Jesus'.

Cosi asked Jesus to fill me with the Holy Spirit. As soon as that happened, it was like a wave came over my entire body. It started from the bottom of my feet up to my head. It was something like a physical touching of God. The way that I like to explain it is like when you are in a car, and

---

[1] See Chapter 34.

suddenly you go over a hill, and your stomach goes up and down. I like that feeling. It was like that but times twenty. That is what it was like, from the bottom of my feet to the top of my head. It was so real and so physical that I have absolutely no doubt that God was touching me. It was the Holy Spirit touching me."

With amazement, she went on to say:

"I was in absolute shock when I fell in the Spirit. I didn't see it coming. I couldn't control it; my muscles didn't exist anymore. I just fell; I was in shock. What it felt like was so unexpected. I did not expect anything like that, even though people were trying to prepare me for it.

I was lying on the floor, in tears and crying. Cosi asked me to praise the Lord, and I did. Then Cosi said 'But not in English'. I was a bit like, 'I don't think I'm going to pray in tongues', but then I felt like something was pushing something out of me. It was coming up, and it just came out. I found myself praising God in tongues, something I thought would never happen to me."

Kristin was awestruck and delighted:

"The whole thing was so beautiful; I felt absolutely at peace. I didn't care that I was lying down. I didn't care that people around me could see me lying down," Kristin added.

The impact of that experience led her to the Blessed Sacrament. It fuelled her desire to be with the Lord and His people forever.

"Eventually, I got the strength to get up and go before the Blessed Sacrament for a long time. I couldn't believe that God touched me so brilliantly, unlike anything before. I couldn't believe that I ever doubted that he existed, and I remember thinking I don't ever want to move on. I wish to remain here forever and want to stay in His presence forever and ever.

I want to be with Him in heaven with my brothers and sisters forever."

"Then Peter said to Jesus, 'Lord, it is good for us to be here; if you wish, I will make three dwellings here, one for you, one for Moses, and one for Elijah,'" (Matthew 4:17).

13

Healings and visions in Magauto

"In the last days it will be, God declares, that I will pour out my Spirit upon all flesh, and your sons and your daughters shall prophesy, and your young men shall see visions, and your old men shall dream dreams,"
(Acts 2:17).

During my visit to Papua New Guinea in November, 2017, I went to a village called Magauto, about two (long) hours' drive from Port Moresby, on terrible roads.

There is a Fellowship of Jesus Covenant community over there. It is only a small fellowship, but the whole village and the neighbouring village came for the seminar. They welcomed us in their beautiful and traditional tribal way.

There were many children there with their families. I felt prompted to tell the story of the children coming to Jesus, how the disciples tried to stop them and how Jesus said to the adults, "Unless you become like little children you will not enter the kingdom of heaven," (Matthew 18:3). One of the girls began to cry and then the girl next to her cried as well. I did not notice them as they were at the back of the church. A member of the team prayed quietly with them.

I shared the Gospel with them. I pointed out that Jesus instructed the disciples not only to proclaim the good news but also to heal the sick.

When I asked who wanted me to pray with them, an older man who seemed like one of their elders, his name was Thomson, came forward and enthusiastically said, "Me, me". I asked him what he would like the Lord to do for him, he said, "My knees, my back and my eyes". I said, "Sure, let's pray for that".

We started by praying over his legs, then his knees and his back. His legs, one which was longer than the other, became balanced. He lifted his knees while standing up and said, "No pain". I asked him to bend over and touch his toes. He did and said, "No pain". I touched his eyes and prayed that Jesus, who gave sight to the blind, would heal his vision. Then I asked him to look at me. "Can you see me?" I asked. He blinked his eyes and said "Yes" and fell to the ground 'resting in the Spirit'. We left him there for a while.

Later in the day everyone gathered in front of his house for fruits and refreshment. Thomson got up and shared in his language what he experienced. All were amazed. Later I asked him to tell me what he shared while his son Jonathon translated.

While Thomson rested in the Spirit, he saw a vision. He saw the clouds open and the hand of God coming through the clouds. People were moving up and down, some coming up and some coming down. "My spirit was going up on the hand of God. As I was going up, I could hear so many different sounds," Thomson related. "From there the Lord spoke to me and said, 'You are okay now, so you go back'.

At that moment in the vision, I found myself in my house, and I went out onto the verandah. The Lord was in the yard reaching out His arms. The Lord was moving closer to me and I was moving closer to Him, trying to hug Him.

In the next vision, I saw a cloud came down and formed all around me up to my neck, just above my neck, and I was praying. While I was praying, there was smoke coming up from where the kitchen is.

Also, while I was praying, I was pleading to the Lord asking him was it right just to leave and die, to give up my ghost and die. I felt it was good for me to give up my ghost and go. From there, I woke up and found myself back in the church."

As we were recording this, I asked Thomson, "When we prayed for you, what did you ask Jesus to do for you?"

"I asked Jesus to clear all the pains; to heal the pain in my legs, knees, back and chest. I had pain in my back for some years and my eyes were not good for some years. I haven't been reading the Bible because I am unable to see it. Now it's all right, and I am looking very true - I can see well."

"You can see well now?" I asked. He replied, "Yes".

His son Jonathon, who was doing the translation, told me he was pleased to see what happened to his father and to see his father giving his testimony. He said that even though his father went to prayer meetings and went to Mass and so on, he was very reserved and did not share his faith publicly.

"A new heart I will give you, and a new spirit I will put within you; and I will remove from your body the heart of stone and give you a heart of flesh," (Ezekiel 36:26).

We also prayed with a woman who seemed to have a hardness and grief in her heart. As we prayed for her, she rested in the Spirit. During that time, she saw a vision. She saw in the sky the word 'ISAIAH', like a big sign but there was no chapter or verse given. She then heard the words, "Lay my word in your heart, lay my word in your heart". When she got up, she felt that the 'stone' was removed from her heart and she received the words, "Follow Jesus and do His ministry". She was uplifted and filled with joy!

The Lord touched many people. He also healed many. There was a young man, 17 years old, who was having problems with his hearing in both ears, and the Lord restored his hearing.

A young 14 year old boy wanted to give his life to Jesus, and he wanted to become a priest, so we prayed for him for that.

Thank you, Lord Jesus, that you continue to move among us caring for the little ones, the poor and humble of heart.

14

Baptised at the River Jordan

"'Look, here is water! What is to prevent me from being baptised?' And Philip said, 'If you believe with all your heart, you may'. And he replied, 'I believe that Jesus Christ is the Son of God'. He commanded the chariot to stop, and both of them, Philip and the eunuch, went down into the water, and Philip baptised him,"
(Acts 8:36-38).

I met Martha during a pilgrimage to the Holy Land. June and Martha are sisters who joined a pilgrimage to the Holy Land with Harvest Pilgrimages (now Harvest Journeys). It was my privilege to have led that pilgrimage. Many received graces and blessings during such pilgrimages.

As I chatted with Martha, she seemed to be a quiet and humble person. In our conversation, she mentioned that her sister, June, was Catholic, but she was not. Assuming that she was a Christian of a different denomination, I asked which church she belonged to.

She said she was Buddhist.

Martha grew up in a Buddhist family. Her sister had become Catholic ten years before. I asked Martha how she was enjoying the pilgrimage, which had just started. She said she was very much enjoying it although it was only in its early days.

I questioned her if she had ever considered becoming Catholic. Martha said yes, as she had attended Catholic schools. However, she hadn't had the opportunity and at the time didn't want to upset her parents, who were devout Buddhists. Her parents have since passed away. I smiled and said, "Perhaps this is your opportunity. In a couple of days, we will be at the River Jordan, and you know what happened there! It's where Jesus was baptised. Perhaps, if you are ready, you could be baptised there?" Martha said, "Oh no, I am not worthy". I responded, "None of us are worthy, but it would be a grace from God to be baptised there".

I left it with her to think it over, and we would chat the next day. Next day we had a long chat. I was hoping to find out how much she knew and understood the Catholic faith and to see whether she indeed was ready to be baptised. I suggested we go through the Creed and see if she had problems with any parts of it. We also had a chat about the role of Our Lady and her place in our Catholic devotions. I was delighted to find out that she had a sincere faith. So, why not have her baptised at the Jordan? Again, she expressed her unworthiness. I spoke with her sister, June, and we decided to approach the pilgrimage chaplain, Fr Ray and asked him to talk to Martha to see if he agreed that she was ready. He too believed she was ready. Fr Ray also raised the question of the legality in Canon Law of baptism at the site. I checked with Fr Hanna (John) Kaldani, who is a canon lawyer and whom I knew in Jordan. Fr Hanna said there was no problem and Fr Ray could issue her baptism certificate on return to Sydney.

We informed Martha that we believed she was ready and that there were no obstacles to her being baptised at the Jordan if she felt she was prepared. We advised her it would be wise to do the Rite of Christian Initiation of Adults (RCIA) program when she returned home, to which she agreed.

The following day, I had a chat with Martha, who seemed to be comfortable with the idea and informed me that she was ready.

We didn't tell any of the pilgrims what was going to happen. We wanted to keep it a surprise for them. However, I told our local guide, Fahdi, what we were planning to do. Fahdi, ever resourceful, procured a candle and a white baptismal gown for the occasion.

That morning we left the hotel on the Dead Sea and travelled to the baptismal site, Al-Maghtas, at Bethany beyond the Jordan. The site is about nine kilometres north of the Dead Sea, and it is the most authentic site where Jesus was baptised. The site is marked with the ruins of the Church of St John the Baptist, a Byzantine church built at the time of Emperor Anastasius (491-518 AD). On the way, we passed by the archaeological area, Tell el-Kharrar, also known as Jabal Mar Elias. Jabal Mar Elias commemorates the place where the prophet Elijah was taken up to heaven on the fiery chariot.

One can sense the holiness of the place. To me, it feels like one of the gateways to heaven. Elijah was taken to heaven, and the Holy Spirit descended upon Jesus after his baptism in the Jordan in the same vicinity.

We celebrated Mass on the side of the river. The pilgrims sat in a shaded amphitheatre with an altar between them and the river. During the Liturgy of the Word, Martha burst out crying from the depths of her heart. Fr Ray quietly approached her and told her that it was okay not to proceed if she was not ready. Martha indicated her willingness to proceed, and it was just that she was touched by the Holy Spirit and was overwhelmed.

During the homily, Fr Ray told everyone what was about to take place. Martha was to be baptised in the faith of our Church and into the Body of Christ. The pilgrims were delighted, and it was my privilege to be her godfather. Martha was baptised at the Jordan; she put on Christ symbolised in the white garment, and a new flame of the light of Christ was lit.

Many pilgrims from the group testified later that it was the highlight of the pilgrimage for them.

After we returned home, Martha wrote to me:

"Thank you again, Costa, for making it possible for me to be baptised at the Jordan River. I don't know why God has blessed me with this great privilege, but I want to tell you that I will do my best to live the rest of my life following in the footsteps of Jesus. I can see you truly live your spirituality, and you are a Christian role model for me. I am honoured to have you as my godfather."

As soon as she returned home, she enquired about the RCIA program and was advised to leave it till the following year as she was planning on visiting her daughter in the United States. However, before she departed, she searched the internet to find a church nearby to her daughter's home to attend Mass.

Martha also wrote:

"Thank you also for being such a supportive, kind and understanding friend throughout the pilgrimage."

June, her sister, wrote to me:

"Dear Costa. I want to thank you very much for playing such a big part in making our pilgrimage so meaningful and enjoyable; you were so generous in sharing your faith, culture and homeland with us and that made our journey so spiritual and personal. We were very fortunate to have you as our tour coordinator for the trip."

June went on to say:

"A very big thank you indeed for the pivotal part you played in clearing the way for Martha to receive Baptism. The Holy Spirit worked through you to make Martha see the way to go. It was such a blessed time for us all. Her own family plus the extended family of our brothers and sisters are delighted with the outcome."

Thank God for all those who nurtured the faith of Martha and prayed for her over the years. I also thank God for using me at the time of the harvest.

"Do you not say, 'Four months more, then comes the harvest?' But I tell you, look around you, and see how the fields are ripe for harvesting. The reaper is already receiving wages and is gathering fruit for eternal life, so that sower and reaper may rejoice together. For here the saying holds true, 'One sows, and another reaps'. I sent you to reap that for which you did not labour. Others have laboured, and you have entered into their labour," (John 4:35-39).

15

Let the children come to me!

"'Let the little children come to me; do not stop them; for it is to such as these that the kingdom of God belongs. Truly I tell you, whoever does not receive the kingdom of God as a little child will never enter it'. And he took them up in his arms, laid his hands on them, and blessed them," (Mark 10:14-16).

It was during the wake after Marie-Josee Rivet's funeral that Lilette shared how grateful she was that Marie had invited her to a Charismatic Healing Mass organised by the Disciples of Jesus Covenant community at St Nicholas of Myra Church in Penrith, Sydney.

Lilette shared:

"About two years ago Marie invited me to go to a Healing Mass at St Nicholas' Church. I went and took with me my grandchildren Amelia and Joshua. Both suffered from extreme asthma. You prayed over us and since then they've never had an asthma attack or had to go to the doctors regarding asthma.

We used to have to go to the hospital very often, especially in winter via ambulance, which cost a lot of money. Since being healed we have not had to go even once."

Anyone who brings someone to Jesus to be healed or to be saved is a real friend. In this case, "Jesus saw their faith," (Luke 5:20) - the child-like faith of Marie and Lilette - and healed the children.

16

Healed and became an instrument of His merciful love

"We do not live to ourselves, and we do not die to ourselves. If we live, we live to the Lord, and if we die, we die to the Lord; so then, whether we live or whether we die, we are the Lord's," (Romans 14:7-8).

Marie-Josee Rivet was a wonderful woman of God. When we met Marie, she had lost her husband. Marie had two children; she lost one of them; the other son was grown up and married with two children.

Marie became a member of the Blue Mountains branch of the Disciples of Jesus Covenant Community. She had a child-like trust in God. She was humble and faithful; she lived our community way of life wholeheartedly.

Before we met Marie, she had suffered from tremendous headaches, and one morning she woke up worse than usual. She went to work and collapsed and was taken to the hospital. The diagnosis was an aneurysm of the right temporal. She lapsed into a coma and for three days she laid in the neuro-intensive care unit.

In a testimony Marie gave, she said:

"I belonged to a Bible study group with Fr Kevin English. My friends were praying for me non-stop. The surgeon told my family I would probably not survive the operation; that the least I could hope for was to be blind and paralysed and would end up in a vegetative state. My husband told the surgeon that Jesus would not desert me. The surgery lasted for eight hours. Throughout those hours, my prayer partners prayed and fasted. Then after the operation the doctor said I would be all right. They continue to praise and thank the Lord."

When Marie returned to good health, she had a lot of time to think:

"Daily I asked the Lord why He had given me a second chance. Then one morning while out walking, I came across Barnardos, a welfare organisation committed to helping children and young people in need. I thought that it would be a good way to evangelise kids and share with them God's love. One thing they have in common is that none of them has heard of God. On the spot, I asked what to do to join and fill out an application form."

The Holy Spirit "who blows wherever he wills" (John 3:8) must have motivated this spontaneous action. It produced plenty of fruits in the lives of many. Marie delighted in fostering children. She fostered over 110 children through Barnardos.

Marie loved children. For many years in spite of her advanced age, she ran in the City to Surf race to raise funds for them.

Her first client was a little Aboriginal boy. Marie wrote: "I took him to church with me. He was distraught to see Jesus on the cross. I didn't see him again for six years until the day of his First Communion. I could see his father was very proud of him. Most of the time, I don't see the result of the seeds I plant and sometimes it takes years to see them."

Marie once wrote: "Recently, I had two little Muslim girls from Pakistan. I brought them to the Disciples of Jesus Community gathering. They were delighted to hear about Jesus, and why he was crucified. The following Sunday at a Community Healing Mass, the elder sister asked for prayer for her mum who was having complications in hospital. A week later, she shared that through Jesus' love, her mum was released from the hospital the very next day. Praise the Lord! The girls talked so much about the Disciples of Jesus Community that they came with their mum on Sunday. Before she and the girls returned to Pakistan, the mother said she was looking forward to attending one more Sunday gathering. The little girls said, 'Mum, they are very good people because they are Christian'."

Marie also worked as a volunteer in a nursing home helping people with paraplegia. Marie recalled: "When I joined the Disciples of Jesus community, I was happy to learn how to evangelise. I met a young man needing my help in a nursing home. His name was Bob, and he had injured himself when at a graduation party and under the influence of alcohol, he dived into a swimming pool. He was angry with God and kept blaming Him for the accident". Marie assured this young man that God loves him, and He was on his side. With God on his side, he could do anything in spite of his injury.

"Six years later, he wanted to see me again, urgently. As we talked, he pointed to the Bible on his table. He said that after I had left, he kept on thinking of what I told him about God. And he decided to give his life to Him. He was certainly not the man I had met six years earlier. He was ready to leave the nursing home, but finance was not available to pay for the alterations needed to his home. I talked to the Disciples of Jesus community, where I belong, and they were very generous. I asked him what he was going to do with his life. Then I suggested that he work with street kids on a farm in Camden, New South Wales. He agreed to give it a go. One Christmas night, he rang me at two o'clock in the morning to tell me of his joy as the kids praised Jesus with him."

A few years later, Marie received the following letter from Bob, the young man who had become a paraplegic.

"Dear Marie,

It is 3.00am, and I can't go to sleep without talking to you.

If my last Christmas was very good, then this one I don't have a word for. I remember you telling me shortly after my accident that if I have a love of God, I can do anything. I laughed at you and wanted to kick you.

Today, eleven years after, your words came back to me. I look around me, and the joy I bring to the kids and parents is very emotional, and I can feel the love of God in each of them. Thank you, Marie. Sorry if I say, 'Thank you'. I know your answer is 'Thank God and not me'. I don't think I would have known God if you were not there in my difficult time. You never say it is easy, but your gentle smile won me over. I don't ever think I am different because I am in a wheelchair.

Sometimes I say to myself there is a reason for everything. If I were okay, I would probably never know God the way I do now. And if it was not for a woman who spent hours comforting and listening to us.

Mum and I send you a Christmas full of joy and an excellent New Year. May God bless you, and my best wishes to the DOJ community. Thank you for your help. Mum and I will never forget the help you gave us when we needed it.

I would like to have the address of the DOJ community in Bali. Maybe one day I will be able to visit them.

My happiness is the present I offer you this Christmas. I know that you are pleased with the way I changed my life.

Thank you, my friend, and may God bless you.

Bob

PS. Remember the day you gave me that letter 12 years ago? I framed it and read it every morning."

Marie spent the rest of her life visiting elderly people, and God used her to heal the loneliness of many. They all loved her. Once they ganged up and told her that one of their friends was sick and would like Marie to visit her. Marie went to visit her that day only to find out that they had prepared a special afternoon tea for her just to thank her for all the care she showed. What a surprise that was!

Marie wrote: "For me, every day, I find that I can help someone to know more about Jesus. My evangelisation is leading souls to discover God."

Marie's main gift was works of mercy. She visited the lonely and elderly, took Communion to the sick, and she also fostered over 110 children for Barnardos. Marie always had stories to tell of sharing her faith and the many positive responses she received.

The following psalm is very much the essence of Marie-Josee:

"O Lord, my heart is not proud nor haughty my eyes. I have not gone after things too great nor marvels beyond me. Truly I have set my soul in silence and peace. As a child has rest in its mother's arms, even so is my soul," (Psalm 131).

17

A love story: God and man

"My beloved speaks and says to me: 'Arise, my love, my fair one, and come away; for now the winter is past, the rain is over and gone,'" (Song of Solomon 2:10-11).

After praying with Mary, I was delighted with the change I saw in her. Before I prayed with her she was scared of being disappointed again. Then after the Lord healed her, she was bubbling with joy and excitement. She was running around telling everyone what happened to her, and on the following day, she gave her testimony publicly. I asked Mary to write it down and pass it to me. She wrote:

"This is about a love story between God and man. A keen lover, pursuing His loved one, wanting to share His divine life with her, wanting to show her how beautiful she is, wanting to free her, heal all her hurts and wipe away all tears from her eyes, wanting her to rest in His love.

My experience of Bathurst Summer School 2011 was all about healing. It was like a love story between God and I – God showed me how real He was and how much He truly loved me. It was the most life-changing and crazy week I've ever experienced!

The Lord worked in me during the week of Summer School. Through the lectures and seminars, I learned of the charismatic gifts. I also learned how to forgive and let go of the things that were stopping me from knowing His love. I was able to forgive someone who had really hurt me in the past, and then hand that person over to God to take care of – this letting go brought me so much closer to God, and I wouldn't have been able to do it if I hadn't attended Summer School.

On the night of baptism in the Spirit, I was prayed with, and when I rested in the Spirit I felt as though I was really falling back into Jesus' arms, and that He was lying there with me, showing me how much He loved me and cared about me. I had always known in my head that God loved me, but this was the first time I had felt it. After I stood up and went to sit in front of the Blessed Sacrament, I could not stop smiling or giggling! As I read Song of Songs, I felt like Jesus was sitting right with me, whispering these lovely things in my ear. I've never felt so loved, and I was on such a high!

Part two of how God showed me His love was on Friday evening. I had enjoyed the night session on Mission and Evangelisation but came out frustrated and angry for some reason. During supper, my friend came to me and said her leg had been healed! One of her legs had been a bit shorter than the other, causing back pain. At the same time, my other friend came to tell me the same thing. Although I was very happy for them, I started to cry because I had terrible back problems due to uneven legs. I had been in and out of hospitals, undergone various treatments and attended every Healing Mass under the sun, but God hadn't healed me. I wondered why these two friends of mine could just get fixed so quickly but I couldn't! They convinced me to go for healing prayer, and I was scared but excited to see if it could work. I explained my situation and then sat in a way that meant I could see one leg was shorter. Almost as soon as the praying began, one of my friends gasped! She burst into tears and said it was growing! I looked down at my feet, and I could see my right leg was getting longer! It was seriously evening up! I sat there, surrounded by awestruck friends watching my leg grow! I was so overwhelmed that I burst into tears and couldn't stop. I hugged everyone and then fell on my knees, so grateful. God was real, and He loved me enough to heal me right in front of my eyes! I stood up and felt taller immediately – it was the most surreal experience of my life, and I ran around telling everyone I saw, occasionally stopping to look at my legs, nice and even.

My relationship with Jesus grew so much on Summer School, and it's now stronger than ever. God is so real, and He loves me. Now I feel like I can go out into the world and show them how good God is by sharing my story."

When we read Mary's reflection that she "attended every healing Mass under the sun but God hadn't healed me", it doesn't mean that God had not heard her prayers, or that the Sacrament of the Healing of the Sick was not efficacious. Sometimes, it is like boiling water. As the temperature rises, we do not see much change with the naked eye, but when the temperature reaches one hundred degrees centigrade the water starts to boil. God hears all our prayers; they all bear fruit.

In the Parable of the Persistent Widow (Luke 18:1-8), Jesus teaches us to be persistent in our prayers. Persistence teaches us patience and trust. If even the most unjust of judges will finally relent in response to the ceaseless petitions then how much more will God – who is, after all, perfect goodness – answer your prayers! Our earnest prayer is pleasing to God. When the Lord 'delays' he does so for a purpose. He is persistent too! When His purpose is achieved then the Lord's answer will be speedy, immediate. So, we never give up. Keep trusting and persevere in prayer.

A genuinely spiritual experience always brings us closer to God. Mary's relationship with God grew, her faith increased, and now she has a story to tell about God's goodness.

18

The peace of Christ came, and insomnia was gone forever

"But the Advocate, the Holy Spirit, whom the Father will send in my name, will teach you everything, and remind you of all that I have said to you. Peace I leave with you; my peace I give to you. I do not give to you as the world gives. Do not let your hearts be troubled, and do not let them be afraid," (John 14:26-27).

Helen (not her real name) was a young woman who attended Summer School several times. I invited her to share what God has done in her life at Summer Schools. Helen shared:

"I had two healings. The first one was when Cosi prayed over me for an ankle injury I had received in early August of the previous year, which I didn't allow to heal properly. I had sustained the injury during a netball accident and aggravated it by playing netball and going to work the next day. It ended up swelling to triple its normal size and was black and blue for about a month-and-a-half before my mother decided I should see a physiotherapist. The physio had said that I had rolled my ankle and done semi-permanent damage to it and I would have to come back twice a week to work on it for a very long time.

I came to Summer School the following January with my ankle still swollen, still slightly bruised and strapped. I asked Cosi to pray for it on Wednesday night, and afterwards, I could stretch it without it hurting, which pleased me. One day later, someone had hurt their ankle and I was asked to get ice for them, and without thinking, I got up and sprinted to the kitchen and back without hurting myself at all. It was the first time I ran in six months."

God had more plans for Helen than healing her ankle. There was an unseen hurt inside her that He wanted to heal.

Helen went on to say:

"The second healing was regarding my insomnia. I suffered from insomnia for most of my life, and I had been on sleeping pills since I was in Year 2. During the baptism in the Holy Spirit, I asked for the gift of peace, and that night as I was resting in the Holy Spirit, I realised I had almost fallen asleep. I got up and went to bed that night, but I didn't take my usual sleeping pills, and slept for seven hours. The night afterwards I went to bed again and slept the whole night. That was the first time I had slept for two days in a row since Year 2."

Helen asked me to pray for the healing of her ankle, but she did not ask for prayer for her insomnia. Helen surrendered her life to the Lord and asked Him to baptise her in the Holy Spirit. She asked the Lord to give her the gift of peace.

Jesus, true to his Word as always, baptised her with the Holy Spirit and gave her His peace. It was in the context of his promise to send the Holy Spirit that Jesus offered us the gift of peace.

19

Bearing witness to the doctor

"Honour the physician with the honour due him according to your need of him, for the Lord created him; for healing comes from the Most High and he will receive a gift from the King," (Ecclesiasticus 38:1-2).

I remember praying with Tommy Donahoe, whom I had known for many years. Tommy was the leader of the Good Shepherd Charismatic Prayer Meeting at Plumpton, Sydney, for many years. He was a very faithful man of God with simple yet strong faith and trust in the Lord.

On 27 May, 2012 he gave the following testimony:

"For many, many months, I suffered severe pain from a pinched nerve on my left hip. I had treatment for it, I had epidurals and many medications, but nothing worked. Then I attended a Healing Mass at Our Lady of the Rosary Church in St Mary's organised by Costandi Bastoli and the Disciples of Jesus Covenant community.

They prayed over me after Mass and almost immediately the pain left.

Shortly after that, I had an appointment with my rheumatologist, and I asked him if he believed in the healing power of prayer. He asked 'Why?', and I told him that I had been to a Healing Mass and had prayers after the Mass and that the pain had left. It hasn't come back since. That was about six months ago, and the pain hasn't come back since. I praise and thank the Lord and thank Costandi and his community."

Tommy was always ready to talk about his beloved Lord. He could not have missed the opportunity to bear witness to his doctor about what the Lord had done for him. Tommy has since passed away and gone home to our Father's house. No doubt, he has now received his ultimate healing. Enjoy the reward of your faith, Tommy.

There is good teaching about healing, health, medicine, doctors and faith in Ecclesiasticus 38:1-14.

20

Car accident, whiplash and then what happened?

"She got up and began to serve him," (Matthew 8:15).

I met Maria (not her real name), a beautiful, young woman in her early twenties at Summer School 2009 at Bathurst. At the time, she worked in youth ministry. Maria told us that she loved her job. She saw it not just as serving the Church and young people but as serving God and the people He loves.

Maria suffered from pain in her neck because of a car accident. A couple of months after Summer School, Maria came to a Charismatic Healing Mass at St Nicholas of Myra Church, Penrith, Sydney. After the Mass, prayer teams prayed for people's individual needs. Maria came to Barbara and I to pray with her. As she told her story, I sensed her deep faith. As we prayed with her, I noticed she was in deep prayer. The Lord answered her prayer instantly.

Maria gave this testimony at the following Charismatic Healing Mass:

"A while ago, a vehicle with a drunk driver ran into the front of my car. My car was so severely damaged that it was going to be written off. Because of the accident I suffered nasty whiplash. I was taken with a neck brace to the hospital by an ambulance. I felt okay at the time, but sometime later, my neck started to hurt badly. I went to my doctor and told him what happened."

Maria went on to say:

"The doctor told me that he had to order another set of x-rays. From the new x-rays, he found that one of the vertebrae in my neck had started to become dislodged. I asked him if there was anything we could do about it because it had started to impinge on my ability to work; sometimes I would have to rest my head for a while because it felt as heavy as a bowling ball and it was difficult to keep it upright. The doctor said that unfortunately there was nothing that he could do. He suggested that I should just rest it and take pain killers. So I did and tried to put up with it. But time went by and it wasn't getting better. Whenever I would feel stressed, I would feel the pain in the same spot in my neck."

Maria continued:

"I went to Summer School at the beginning of 2009 where I met Costandi and the Disciples of Jesus Covenant community. Sometime afterwards, I went to a Charismatic Mass where I went for prayer. The prayer team asked what I would like Jesus to do for me. I said my neck hurts badly and sometimes I can't even do my work because I must rest it. I would like God if it is His will to take the pain away. So they prayed for that. As they prayed, suddenly, I felt heat going up and down my neck as if someone was touching my neck and straightening all the bones of my neck. After they had finished praying, I told them what I had felt and told them that I believe Jesus healed me but that I would let them know in a couple of weeks.

After a couple of weeks, I rang Costandi, and I told him that I hadn't felt my neck hurt since, even when I felt stressed. This healing has strengthened my relationship with God."

Maria declared: "I believe that God can do anything. Praise God because He is the Healer."

Thinking of this testimony reminds me of the story of Jesus healing Peter's mother-in-law. I know there are many jokes about this miracle; I am not thinking of that! I am thinking of where it says that she got up and served them. Maria, like Peter's mother-in-law, loved Jesus and wanted to serve Him. Thus motivated, she came to Him to be healed. Would Jesus say no to that? I am not saying that Jesus healed because He wanted her to serve Him. He healed her because He too loved her and wanted to fulfil her desire to love and serve Him.

"When Jesus entered Peter's house, he saw his mother-in-law lying in bed with a fever; he touched her hand, and the fever left her, and she got up and began to serve him. That evening they brought to him many who were possessed with demons; and he cast out the spirits with a word and cured all who were sick," (Matthew 8:14-16).

21

Freed from pain, sickness and rejection

Louise (not her real name) came for prayer for a physical problem, the healing of her back. When she received that healing, she was encouraged to ask for more, for her respiratory problems. The Lord however, had more healings in mind for her. She is loved; He loves her; she is His daughter. He has a future full of hope for her.

Louise gave the following testimony:

"My name is Louise. My main problem was lower back pain which was affecting the sciatic nerve and I was having pain radiating down my right leg. I had it for about three or four years. I've received treatment from a physiotherapist to whom I was referred by my doctor. I've taken anti-inflammatory medication and had massages regularly as well. Yesterday I received prayer with Cosi. When we prayed, I could see that my legs were out of alignment and then there was some movement occurring. I had a sense of just complete peace. After the prayer I was pain-free.

I also asked for prayer for my sinuses. I had a lot of problems with hay fever and a sensitive respiratory tract. I'm prone to a bit of bronchitis and respiratory tract infections.

During the prayer session I was given a word from the Lord: 'I will never forget you, I have carved you on the palm of my hand... does a mother forget her baby or a woman the child within her womb? Yet even if these forget I will never forget you,' (Isaiah 49:15, 16). I felt a tremendous peace and just a complete acceptance from God and an overwhelming sense of being loved and knowing my right as His daughter, a daughter of the King, and that I'm his princess.

Now, I have no feeling of rejection or fear about the future either. I feel my heavenly Father knows my needs and He will provide for me.

I've always been well-liked with regards to family and friends, but I've always had a fear of rejection. I couldn't understand why I've had that feeling because I come from a very warm family and had been brought up in a really lovely community and parish and had a lot of friends throughout my life. But I think from my experience more recently I've been a bit fearful of being alone, but I don't have that sense of being alone anymore."

This is what our God is like. He always wants to give us more than we dare to ask for.

You are God's dream come true!

"Before I formed you in the womb, I knew you," (Jeremiah 1:5).

22

How Mel was healed from menstrual complications

"And behold, a woman who had suffered from a haemorrhage for twelve years came up behind him and touched the fringe of his garment; for she said to herself, 'If I only touch his garment, I shall be made well'. Jesus turned, and seeing her, he said, 'Take heart, daughter; your faith has made you well'. And instantly the woman was made well," (Matthew 9:20-23).

As Mel testifies, menstrual complications can be very debilitating. To be healed from them is a life-changing experience.

Mel gave the following testimony at Bathurst Summer School around 2011:

"I was nauseous and sick during my menstrual cycle every month for about a year, and it was quite debilitating. I was going to lots of specialists; I went to about three different GPs. They gave me several different diagnoses, none of which helped.

Then at Summer School I was prayed over and I rested in the Holy Spirit. It was a very emotional time for me and I cried a lot. After returning home from Summer School I didn't quite comprehend what had happened; I was still processing it for quite some time. Then came the time for my next cycle, and I found that I had no nausea, and I wasn't vomiting; the Lord healed me, and I've been fine ever since."

Mel said that it was a very emotional time for her, and she cried a lot. We should not be afraid of our emotions. Our emotions are a gift from God. It is okay to cry. "Jesus shed tears," (John 11:35).

Sometimes we do not see the result of our prayer on the spot. We continue to trust that our Father has heard our prayers. Mel did not know what God had done for her while she rested in the Spirit until her following period.

23

Vanessa was diagnosed with hydrocephalus and then a brain tumour. What happened next...

"As you also join in helping us by your prayers, so that many will give thanks on our behalf for the blessing granted us through the prayers of many,"
(2 Corinthians 1:1).

I met Vanessa when she came for a personal prayer ministry at Summer School in 2009. After Summer School, Vanessa came to our monthly Healing Masses at St Nicholas of Myra, Penrith, Sydney, for two or three months. Each time she attended a Healing Mass she would go forward for prayer ministry.

At the time she was under medical care following being diagnosed in 2001 with hydrocephalus, which is a build-up of fluid on the brain. The excess fluid puts pressure on the brain which can damage it. Vanessa had several operations. In 2008, after routine checks, she was diagnosed with a brain tumour. They operated on her and removed seventy-five percent of the tumour. Mercifully, the tumour was not cancerous.

To get rid of the rest of the tumour she had radiation. The radiologist advised her that the best result they could hope for would be that the tumour would stop growing and spreading.

Following the treatments, Vanessa went for routine checks. Later in 2009, Vanessa testified:

"During the first six months I had a routine check, and there was no change and no growth, which was a good result. Then I went to Summer School in January 2009, and I was prayed over for healing. I've been to several Healing Masses, I've had family and friends pray for me for the tumour to be completely gone.

I recently had a routine check. Thank God, the specialist informed me that there is no evidence of the tumour. The Lord has healed me! I give praise to God!"

I have recently been in touch with Vanessa, 10 years later, and she still gives thanks to God for her healing and continues to inspire others with her testimony, giving all glory to God.

Vanessa's perseverance and faith were rewarded. No doubt her family, friends and all those who prayed with and for Vanessa's healing have rejoiced with her and given thanks to the Lord for her healing.

"You also must help us by prayer, so that many will give thanks on our behalf for the blessing granted us through the prayers of many," (2 Corinthians 1:11).

"And when [Jesus] saw [the paralysed man's friends'] faith he said, 'I say to you, rise, take up your bed and go home,'" (Luke 5:20, 24).

24

Signs and wonders – Port Moresby, 2011

"He sent them out to preach the kingdom of God and to heal the sick," (Luke 9:2).

Paul Miamel, the leader of the Port Moresby branch of the Disciples of Jesus Covenant Community, invited me to conduct healing seminars in Port Moresby, Papua New Guinea in May, 2011. It was my first visit to Papua New Guinea.

I chose the title 'Jesus Heals Us' as I felt the focus should be on Jesus, not healing. The aim was to proclaim the good news and to witness that Jesus heals today, and also to teach others how to minister God's healing love to those in need.

Jude Besterwich, a friend, offered to accompany me at his own expense. He was a great companion for the mission and the Lord used him a powerful way.

We arrived at Port Moresby Airport and to our surprise we found a committee waiting to welcome us. Led by Paul and his wife Anne Marie, Peter and Agnes and three other 'mothers' (older women in the community) met us. The mothers wore special matching dresses made with the colours representing our logo, and they presented us with leis and traditional hats.

They took us on a tour of downtown Port Moresby. We travelled in the cabin of a utility vehicle. The rest of the party sat in the back of the ute. I felt uneasy as I thought the mothers should travel in the cabin, but they insisted on sitting in the back of the ute. Only on the last day, at our insistence, were we allowed a ride in the back of the vehicle.

On the evening of the first day, they invited us out for dinner with Archbishop (now Cardinal) John Ribat MSC and the members of the Disciples of Jesus Covenant Community Branch Council. It was an enjoyable evening. I was struck by the friendliness of the Archbishop. At the end of our time together, His Grace gave us his blessing.

The community in Port Moresby was initially expecting 50-100 people to attend. The number on the first night was about 100 people, which increased on the second night to about 150 and 300 by the third night.

People from the community and its related fellowships (outreaches) came in force. Many stayed at the home of Paul and Anne Marie like a large, happy family.

The seminar took place at St Peter Chanel Parish Hall. Many parishioners and members of the Legion of Mary, the Rosa Mystica and Divine Mercy prayer groups also attended.

The community and its related fellowships had prepared for this event for five weeks with prayer, fasting, novenas, and Life in the Spirit seminars[1]. On the weekend

---
[1] See Chapter 38.

before the seminars, they took the young people on retreat to the top of a high mountain for prayer and fasting. The young people were prohibited from taking mobiles, radios or anything that would be a distraction. Their meals on the weekend consisted of two biscuits for dinner, one biscuit for breakfast and one biscuit for lunch.

In an email to me just before I departed Sydney, one of the leaders, Leslie Kolis, wrote, "We have been praying and fasting for some time. We just held a Life in the Spirit seminar weekend for our young people as part of our spiritual preparation for the program. There is a Holy Spirit fire burning now in the hearts of many, especially our young people, who will play some important roles during the program".

In Australia, our Blue Mountains branch and the Tehillah Community, Blacktown, Sydney, which was led by Jude, also supported this event with their prayers and intercession.

The Holy Spirit filled the atmosphere at the seminars with His presence. The expectant faith of the participants was very high. Their prayer, praise and worship were anointed. The participants were free in their exuberant praise and their dancing to the Lord.

We prayed with over 30 people for the gift of healings. I invited people to pray with those who needed healings, and the Lord healed many. Among those who received the gift of healings were two girls about 12-13 years. After receiving the gift, they prayed with a couple of people, and the Lord healed those people. One of them was Janet who had a problem with one of her elbows; since childhood when her brother hit her with a stick she was unable to stretch her arm fully. After the two youngsters prayed with her, Janet gained full mobility of the injured elbow. The Lord also healed her of a back problem.

Many gave testimony that the Lord healed them during the seminars:

Michael suffered terrible back pain for about a year. He said that it was so bad that he had to ask his wife to do everything for him, including cutting hands of bananas from trees. He felt sorry for the burden that he was for his wife. He had prayed very hard to the Lord to heal him, but it did not happen. When we prayed for Michael on the first night, he said it felt like his back was washed, it felt cold. The pain left him and he was delighted.

Christophilda had a chronic wrist injury which left her with minimal movement. She was unable to do her housework properly as she could not put pressure on her wrist. She said that the doctor told her that there was nothing more that could be done to help her. After we prayed with her, she recovered fully and had free movement at her wrist. When she got up to give her testimony, she continuously rotated her wrist again and again with no pain whatsoever.

Celestine had a nodule on the thyroid gland in her neck. As we prayed with her she forgave people who had hurt her. She experienced inner healing, and the nodule disappeared completely.

Mary had a problem with the left side of her body with one breast larger than the other. She also had a problem with her knees. For several years she had been unable to kneel at the church. In the 12 months before the seminar, she went to see the doctor three times and underwent many tests, but he could not help her. She mentioned that the teaching on inner healing touched her. Afterwards, she reflected on her life, trying to go to the root cause of her problems. She believed that the Lord would heal her. On the following day, as she was coming up for prayer, she felt the presence of Jesus and sensed the Holy Spirit blowing through her. Mary felt that her bones were moving like when the wind blows over a leaf and blows it away. She believed it was at that moment that the Lord healed her. When Mary went home, she looked at herself in the mirror and discovered that both her breasts were equal in size. The Lord also healed her knees, and she was able to kneel, demonstrating it on the stage.

Genevieve, from a fellowship based at Biotou, two and a half hours drive from Port Moresby, was attending the seminar. During the evening, she received a phone call from her village and learned that her mother had fallen on steps and was unconscious. She had the sense to call the people around her to pray. While we were all praying she received another phone call from the village to say that her mother had recovered consciousness.

After attending a wedding on Saturday morning, Rose (Shrebecca), who was pregnant, was riding on the back of a utility vehicle when it was involved in an accident. She was hit badly on the side of her stomach by her sister's knee. She also bruised her arm and shoulder. She was in shock and the baby was not moving. Immediately after I prayed with her, she could feel the baby moving, and the Lord healed her arm and shoulder.

When her time came Rose gave birth to a beautiful baby girl. They named her Antonia. I met Antonia and have witnessed her growing as I have visited the community in Papua New Guinea over the past five years. Antonia is a special girl and loves Jesus. The last time I saw her she came and asked me to pray that the Lord may bless her.

Virginia had a partial hearing problem and could not hear from a distance. After prayer she was able to hear her husband speaking softly, five to six metres away!

Virginia's sister, Rachael, also had hearing loss in one ear. Sometimes she could hear but with an echo and sometimes she couldn't hear at all. She also had a back problem. After we prayed with her she could hear clearly and continuously, and the pain in her back was gone.

Genevieve, a 13 year old young woman, was scared of the dark. Every night she would wake up frightened and turn on the lights and disturb the whole family as they all slept in the same room. After we prayed over her, she was healed and slept through the entire night. Her father said that it was a blessing for all the family!

The Lord worked many more healings, both physical and inner healings. In one count, 24 people received cures for back injuries and unbalanced legs. Someone estimated that the number of people who received healings during the three days was between 75 and 100 people.

Following such a busy weekend, on Monday night the community met together to farewell us as we were leaving on the Tuesday morning. What a farewell it was with food, hymns, spiritual songs, dances and expressions of brotherly love and exchanges of gifts.

On my subsequent visits I have reconnected with many of the people I mentioned above. They continue to praise the Lord for the healings they have received. All praise and glory to our Lord who saves.

25

Vivienne forgave her husband

Vivienne shared this testimony at a Charismatic Mass in May 2014:

"My name is Vivienne, and I'm happy to attend this seminar. I was touched yesterday when Costandi was sharing about the inner memory healing experienced by his wife. I have lived with my husband being violent to me. I had never forgiven him for all the abuse he had been doing to me and my kids. During the prayer for healing, I cried my heart out because Jesus healed me. I forgave him for all the violence he had committed against me throughout the eighteen years of our marriage. I want to thank God for the healing I received on Saturday. I feel free and released with the grace of God. Amen!"

26

The lame walk, the blind see, and the deaf and dumb hear and speak

"Lord, enable your servants to speak your word with complete boldness as you stretch out your hand to heal and perform signs and wonders through the name of your holy servant Jesus," (Acts 4:29).

What happened in Mount Hagen, Papua New Guinea in 2018 was truly amazing. I was invited by the Catholic Charismatic Renewal there to speak and minister at three successive conferences in three deaneries of Mount Hagen; namely Banz, Mun and Karipia.

After praying about it I accepted the invitation. Tony Bittar, a brother from our Sydney South branch of the Disciples of Jesus Covenant Community, accompanied me. I am grateful for his brotherly company, his care and support and his ministry.

On our arrival in Mount Hagen we went to visit Archbishop Douglas Young and received his blessings. Then we travelled from one location to the other. In each of the areas, the local chiefs together welcomed us in their colourful, traditional, tribal way. Hundreds of people lined up along the roads to greet us. I was delighted to see not only the Catholic Christians, but also Pentecostal and Lutheran believers and others welcomed and fully participated in the conferences.

The preparations were massive, both physically and spiritually. Land had to be cleared, marquees erected, and in Mun, they also dug a toilet for us! The Catholic Charismatic leaders in Mount Hagen prayed and interceded. I and so many supporters here in Australia did the same.

The word went out, and many people began to long for our coming. This was my fourth visit to Mount Hagen. Many travelled on foot from the surrounding villages to get to the conference centres. Until you have been there it is difficult to imagine their poverty and very basic lifestyle. Yet the level of the expectant faith of many of them was very high.

We heard the story of a woman who was bedridden for four years. She prayed and prayed to be able to attend. On the first day of the conference she got out of bed and walked to the conference. The Lord healed her on the way.

At each of the locations we proclaimed the basic Gospel message. We spoke about the Father's love and the death and resurrection of Jesus and prayed with them for baptism in the Holy Spirit. Hundreds were baptised in the Holy Spirit and received the gift of tongues and other gifts.

Then we spoke about Jesus our healer. We focused on the scriptures that say, "By his wounds, we have been healed," (Isaiah 53:5). Then, with the local leaders, we prayed for people, that the Lord would heal them. We saw many healed in many different ways. We saw the lame walk, the blind recover their sight and the deaf hear. All the glory belongs to our Lord Jesus, our healer.

Let me share with you some of the miraculous healings that took place.

The Crippled Man

I prayed with a man who was crippled. He was seated on one of the steps of the stage. People were sitting around him praying for him, and some were waiting for prayer too. I did not know much about him. After I prayed over him, I blessed him with the cross. Then I found myself taking him by the hand, and I said, "Let us walk". Without hesitation, he got up and walked. He let go of my hand and walked on his own. I encouraged him to keep going, which he did. The people young and old cheered and clapped their hands, giving glory to God. I asked him to follow me to the stage. He did. He climbed the stairs onto the stage without assistance, even though the steps were a bit higher than usual. Again, the crowds cheered and clapped.

He gave his testimony: "I used to go to Fatima school. In 1980 I had an accident when I was playing soccer. I hurt my hip bone. I have been crippled for 38 years."

The people again cheered and clapped in amazement.

He continued: "I used to go along the streets and in town with sticks. People laughed at me, and sometimes they gave money, sometimes they helped me, sometimes they made a fool of me. Now I am well. Now I thank the Lord for sending His servants to Banz to heal us."

The people cheered again. "Now me talk big thank you for Jesus," he added. They all rejoiced.

A lame man walks

During one of the sessions, a leader asked me to pray with a man who was seated on a chair. He told me that the man was crippled. I asked the crippled man: "What would you like Jesus to do for you?" He replied, "I want to walk".

As I prayed with him, I felt a prompting to bless him with the cross. I blessed him on his head, shoulders, chest and back, on his thighs, knees and calves. Then I put my hand out to him to help him to stand. He thought I was shaking hands with him so he started shaking my hand. I held his hand and I said, "Stand". He did.

"Could you do this before? Could you stand up?" I asked. "No," he replied. "Let us walk," I said encouragingly. He started to walk while holding my hand. After going in a circle, I said to him, "I now want you to let go of my hand and walk towards me". He did so more confidently with each step.

Later, I encouraged him to give his testimony.

"What is your name?" I asked, holding the microphone for him. "Simon," he said, "my name is Simon".

"How long you have been unable to walk?" I asked. "One and a half years," he replied. "One and a half years, you said, and this is the first time you walked in one and a half years?" I asked. "Yes, one and a half years," he replied.

"Who healed you?" I asked. "Jesus... in the name of Jesus," he replied. The crowds were delighted and praised the Lord.

"And by faith in his name, his name itself has made this man strong whom you see and know, and have the faith that is through Jesus," (Acts 3:16).

I remember praying with another man who was able to walk only with walking sticks. After we prayed with him he walked without any assistance. He carried one of the sticks on his shoulder, like a soldier carrying his gun, and roamed freely.

"I was blind now I can see."

One of the leaders took me to a man who was blind. I asked the blind man, "What would you like Jesus to do for you?" He said he wanted to see.

I asked him, "Can you see anything now?" He answered as he looked at the sky, "I can see only light, white light".

I prayed for him, asking Jesus who is the Light of the World to heal him. I touched his eyelids as he closed his eye; I could feel the pupils move. When I had finished praying, I asked him if he could see anything. He looked up at the sky. I said "Look at my face, what can you see?" The man replied, "I can see your glasses".

"What about the rest of my face?" I asked. He said, "Not clear".

I prayed over his eyes again. Again I said, "Look at me, what can you see?" He answered, "Yes, I can see your face," and his face lit up.

"Can you see me?" I asked. "Yes, yes," he answered with excitement in his voice. "Can you see the stage?" I asked, to make sure that he had received his full sight back, as the stage was about six metres away. "Yes, yes, I can see the stage," he answered enthusiastically.

"Is everything clear?" I asked. "Yes, clear," he replied emphatically.

Then we walked to the stage. I asked the people to give us their attention. He took the microphone and simply said: "Thank you, Jesus. I was blind, and now I can see". The crowd cheered. Then he went on to explain that he has been blind for two years. He finished by saying: "Thank you, Jesus. Amen".

A woman blind in one eye

There was a woman who was blind in one eye; her name was Maria and she came from Banz parish. She was a Communion Minister and a leader in the Legion of Mary. She had lost sight in one of her eyes which interfered in her daily life in many ways. After three years she went to her doctor who was not able to help her. That was three years before the conference. Maria then confirmed that she had been blind in one eye for a total of six years.

Maria testified, "I used to see only with one eye, but yesterday they put their hands over my head and prayed for Jesus and He healed me, and now I can see with the other eye. I can see the people around me with both eyes".

"For with you is the fountain of life; in your light, we see light," (Psalm 36:9).

What happened to a seven year old boy?

One of the leaders took me to pray with a seven year old boy who was with his mother. He was deaf and dumb.

After I prayed with him and blessed him with the cross, I placed my hand on the left-hand side behind his head and clicked my fingers. He turned his head. I did the same on the other side. He also responded. I repeated this again and again; every time he responded by clicking his fingers. I offered him the cross to kiss, which he did.

Then I asked him to say "Jesus". He heard me and said "Jesus" very faintly, with his face beaming with joy. Someone shouted, "He can speak!" I raised my voice, "One, two, three". The people clapped three times and shouted, "Jesus, mighty King!" giving glory to the Lord who makes the deaf hear and the dumb speak.

I interviewed the boy's mother:

Costandi: "What is the boy's name?"

The mother: "Eskimo".

Costandi: "How old is Eskimo?"

The mother: "Seven years".

Costandi: "Seven years? And he hasn't been able to hear or speak all his life?"

The mother: "Yes. Since birth".

Costandi: "And now he could hear us clicking? Yes?"

The mother: "Yes".

Costandi: "And he could say Amen?"

The mother: "Yes".

Costandi: "And when I said 'Jesus', he said, 'Jesus'?"

The mother: "Yes".

Costandi: "Could he do that before?"

The mother: "Before he could only say 'Ma, ma' but not Jesus".

Costandi: "What is your name?"

The mother: "Chris".

Costandi: "Surname?"

Chris: "Timothy".

Costandi: "From where?"

Chris: "From Banz, from here".

I said to Eskimo: "You are a great boy! Give me a hug!"

Climbing Mount Israel, a prayer mountain

On the first morning at Mun parish, having given two talks, Tony and I were hoping to have a lunch break. Instead, people there were waiting to take us up to their prayer mountain. They called it Mount Israel.

As we started our climb they insisted that I lead. I was already tired. At the foot of the mountain they had erected a shelter that was designated as a Reconciliation shelter. This was where people come to meet the priest and celebrate the Sacrament of Reconciliation. I persevered three-quarters of the way but then I needed to rest. So I stood aside and encouraged the rest to go on. It was a good reminder that I was advancing in age. The view was picturesque and inspiring. A young man came to assist me climbing the rest of the way.

A short distance from there we came to a hut. That was the hut where the men met for prayer. Another excuse for a rest. We stopped and had a short prayer time.

Finally, we reached the top. There was a bigger hut where the women prayed. Outside the hut we received some refreshments then we entered the hut to pray. They asked Tony and I to call God's blessings on the place and all the people there. It was an anointed moment. The beauty and simplicity of the site and the richness of their faith touched me.

Tony gave them the gift of a Rosary from the Holy Land that had been blessed on Calvary and the Holy Sepulchre during our pilgrimage the previous year.

What happened to Anda, Pastor Simon's father?

On the way down a man came to my assistance. He was Pastor Simon of the Assemblies of God. We had a blessed time sharing our faith.

Back at the foot of the mountain, we sat to have some lunch. Pastor Simon introduced me to his father Anda, who was helping there. Simon told me that his father was in constant pain following an injury to his back when he had fallen off a tree, which I think occurred about 17 years ago. Simon asked if I would pray over his father. I hesitated, thinking that if people see me praying over him, many will line up for prayer, and I wasn't ready for that. I prefer to proclaim the Gospel, pray with the people to open up to the power of the Holy Spirit and then pray for healing. I noticed a hall not far from where we were sitting. I asked Simon to ask his dad to meet us at the hall. There we prayed privately with his dad, and the pain left him completely. Simon's dad was the first to give his testimony on the following day during the healing service.

Teachers came for prayer

On another occasion, at midday when we were about to take a lunch break, a local leader came to me on the stage. He informed me that all the teachers from the local school were coming for prayer. Since they only had a short break he suggested that we pray over them as a group. I readily agreed.

They came and stood in front of the stage. I stretched my arms over them and began in praising and thanking the Lord for their openness and their faith.

I felt a lot of their burdens. I prayed whatever came to mind. As I did, I was looking at them. They all bowed their heads, and many of them were noticeably in prayer. Then I saw a female teacher crying and reaching for her handkerchief. I felt a special anointing and continued to pray until the Lord lifted the burden off me.

The teachers thanked me. They were very grateful, and so was I.

Very encouraging feedback

The conference at Kiripia was cut short due to a member of the community having passed away before our arrival and the funeral being delayed as the family were awaiting the arrival of other relatives.

As a result, a teacher from the local primary school, Joseph Lama, offered to drive us back to Mount Hagen. He was very grateful for the opportunity. He was very excited and wanted to talk about his experience and did so as he drove.

When he began sharing, I took the opportunity to record what he said:

"The two days you spent with us were wonderful and powerful. The whole community felt the presence of Jesus in every session, and even to the extreme in the healings that took place. It was so powerful. The Lord healed many from different types of diseases and sickness; many backaches were healed, and many recovered their hearing and sight. That's an extraordinary experience for almost everyone in the community. It was so inspiring."

I asked Joseph to tell me how this affected him personally. He said, "One of the things that I learned is the importance of using the Scriptures in the presentations. You used Scripture references to every point made. I felt as though Jesus Christ was physically present and speaking to me.

For me, as a teacher participating in the event, it was so exciting, like seeing and hearing Jesus physically. It was great nourishment for my faith as a follower of Jesus, someone who loves Jesus and who wants to live with Jesus.

Personally, I felt it was an extraordinary encounter, especially in the healing process. I now believe in the words: 'By His (Jesus') wounds, we are healed,' (Isaiah 53:5). By His wounds on the Cross, we are healed. Something so precious in my life. Whenever I pray from now on, I will remember the wounds of Jesus. Whether I am praying for myself or anyone in my family or friends, I will remember the wounds of Jesus."

Then I asked, "Tell me about your experience with the Holy Spirit".

Joseph replied, "One of the sessions that I felt was so important to me was the one on baptism in the Holy Spirit. I used to think that as someone who was born into the Catholic Church, baptised at childhood, I had already received the Holy Spirit, and that's it. But in this session, I realised that I need to renew my baptismal vows, surrender my life and experience baptism in the Spirit to empower me to be a faithful Christian. So, the session on baptism in the Holy Spirit was crucial to me".

Joseph asked me to email him notes from the teachings I gave. I was pleased to do so as I felt he would make good use of them.

"While God also bore witness by signs and wonders and various miracles and by gifts of the Holy Spirit distributed according to his own will," (Hebrews 2:4).

27

The Lord hears the cry of the poor

"Listen, my beloved brothers and sisters. Has not God chosen the poor in the world to be rich in faith and to be heirs of the kingdom that he has promised to those who love him?" (James 2:5).

During my visit to the Philippines in August, 2018, I spent most of my time with Fr Paul Uwemedimo, a Missionaries of God's Love priest and a member of the Disciples of Jesus Covenant Community. Carine Cesar from Melbourne joined us for a few days.

We spent a lot of time in the impoverished slum areas of Carlife and Payatas in Quezon City, Manila, where Fr Paul conducts his ministry. The living conditions there are heartbreaking. At times we were overwhelmed feeling the brokenness amidst a broken society. The children are suffering, and the youths burdened. How can poverty be so flagrant? There is darkness on so many levels. However, Jesus the Light of the World is with them.

On the first day, to my surprise, we had Mass at the Careers Executive Services Board (a Government Board). Fr Paul invited me to share about my experience at Papua New Guinea. I showed them a short video of the lame man who was healed at Mount Hagen (his story is in the previous chapter) and spoke about expectant faith.

After Mass we prayed with many and the Lord healed them:

Don had a frozen shoulder, Carmen suffered from hypertension, Joanna had upper and lower back pain, Ursy had lumbar scoliosis and cervical spondylosis while Carmela suffered from extreme back pains. The Lord healed them all!

One of the girls said she felt like she was in heaven.

Darius came to me and said that he was suffering from prostate pain, and as I was praying with the others, his pain disappeared.

And so on.

After we prayed with everybody that needed prayer, Fr Paul blessed the new office as well.

I spoke about and prayed for healing at five or six Masses during my visit as the Lord Jesus stretched his mighty arm and healed many.

After sharing with seven of the youth leaders on how to pray for healings, a young woman who had back and neck pain and was feeling sick all over walked in. They asked me to pray over her. I said, "It's your turn". So, they prayed with her, and the Lord healed her instantly.

The following day the youth leaders prayed with more sick people and the Lord healed them. They prayed with an older woman who was healed and also felt a touch from the Holy Spirit all over her body.

Indeed, the Lord hears the cry of the poor. Hallelujah!

28

A season of Pentecost at Mount Hagen!

"The Spirit of the Lord is upon me, because he has anointed me to proclaim good news to the poor,"
(Luke 4:18).

Healings and signs at the celebration of the 30th anniversary of Catholic Charismatic Renewal, Mount Hagen, Papua New Guinea.

In October 2017, I was invited by the Catholic Charismatic Renewal to speak and to minister at their 30th anniversary in Mount Hagen, Papua New Guinea.

At the beginning of the conference, we celebrated who we are in God. We celebrated that we are sons and daughters of God, that we are His work of art created in Christ Jesus to do the good works that He has assigned for us.

Then I shared with them my experience at the Golden Jubilee of the worldwide Catholic Charismatic Renewal on the eve of Pentecost in Rome, 2017. I shared how the pope encouraged us to praise the Lord and not to be afraid of expressing our joy. Pope Francis said, "Exultation, happiness, joy! That is the fruit of the working of the Holy Spirit! Either a Christian experiences joy in his or her heart or something is wrong". But they didn't need much encouragement because they were quite open to praise the Lord with joy.

Then we focused on Jesus and his mission.

"The Spirit of the Lord is upon me, because he has anointed me to proclaim good news to the poor. He has sent me to proclaim freedom for the prisoners and recovery of sight for the blind, to set the oppressed free, to proclaim the year of the Lord's favour," (Luke 4:18-19).

After proclaiming Jesus and his mission, a time of ministry followed, and Jesus healed many.

Several people came for prayers for pain or problems with their back. When this happens, I usually check the length of their legs to see if one appears longer than the other, which is something that can occur because of a twist in the spine or pelvis. Checking their legs in this way helps me to know when they are healed and when to stop praying. Usually that takes a few minutes. As we pray for them, their legs become balanced, and when they stand up, they find that they are free from pain.

Lame child

A lady came with a child, a three year old girl. She told us that the child wasn't able to walk. I understood that she had never crawled so there must have been something seriously wrong with her. As we prayed, I felt moved to bless the child's

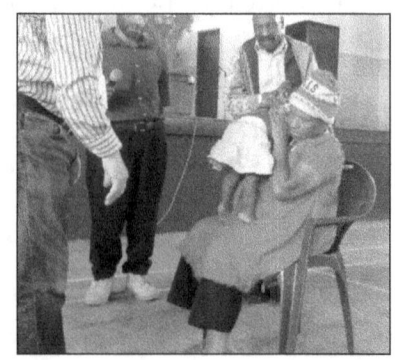

legs with a cross I brought with me from Jerusalem, which had been blessed on Calvary and the Holy Sepulchre of our Lord.

The Cross of Jesus has become the tree of life for us.

I had already spoken about the power of the Cross of Jesus. While we were praying, the child started to cry and then began to kick with her legs and eventually stood firmly on the lady's lap,  which indicated that something had happened. Seeing that the child was now able to stand up, I encouraged the lady to take her home and teach her how to walk. Later that evening, the mother came back to testify that the child was now walking with assistance.

Healing of hardened hearts

During one of the sessions, I spoke about unforgiveness. I explained that when people refuse to forgive or are unable to forgive, this can always be a significant obstacle for them receiving healing from the Lord.

While I was talking about this, I noticed many people were very uncomfortable. I invited people to come forward

if they were having difficulty in forgiving others. A large number came forward.

I explained that forgiveness is a decision that we make using our will even if we are still hurting. We are to forgive as God has forgiven us in Christ (Ephesians 4:32).

If we don't forgive, we are making ourselves into judges and usurping Jesus' role. God can give us the grace and the power to forgive; however, we make the decision. I explained that I would pray a general prayer asking the Lord to give us the grace to choose to forgive, then I would bless them with a cross that was blessed on Calvary where all our sins were forgiven. I suggested that they make their decision as I blessed them with the cross.

I prayed and blessed them individually with the cross asking each time, "Do you forgive?", "Do you forgive?", "Do you forgive?" Every one of them said "Yes". The Holy Spirit was working in a mighty way softening their hearts.

God is always ready to give us the grace and the power to forgive.

I am reminded of the time several years ago when I was leading a Harvest Journeys pilgrimage to the Holy Land. On our first stop in Jordan we visited the ancient Nabatean city of Petra. I love Petra. In Petra, we had over half a day's visit on foot and then gave the rest of the day for the pilgrims to enjoy the site at leisure. One of the pilgrims chose to accompany me during that time. We talked about many things, including the ministry of healing in the Catholic Charismatic Renewal. I mentioned that unforgiveness is the biggest obstacle that prevents people from receiving their healing from the Lord. Yet it is challenging for people to forgive at times.

She indicated that was her story. She had been unable to forgive someone who hurt her over 35 years ago. She knew all the reasons why she should forgive but found it very difficult to do it. I pointed out that forgiveness is a decision we make with our will despite our feelings. Then when our emotions get stirred up again by the hurtful memories, we remind ourselves that we have made our decision to forgive, and eventually our emotions learn to let go. We are then set free. I asked my fellow pilgrim if she would like me to pray with her for the grace to make that decision to forgive the person who hurt her. She said she didn't mind.

So, among the ancient ruins of Petra we prayed, and God gave her the grace and she made her decision. The ancient wound was healed and she was set free. Twice during the pilgrimage she thanked me and told me how grateful she was to the Lord for setting her free. She said that her decision opened the door for the many graces she experienced during the pilgrimage.

Grateful Nathan

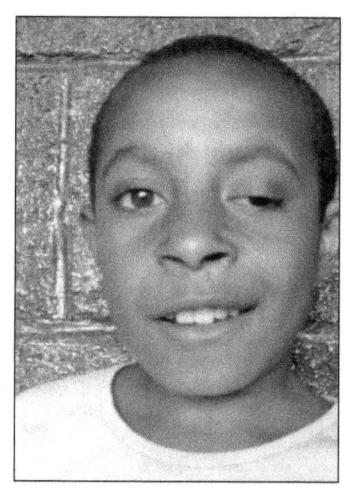

Back to Mount Hagen. During the break I went outside the hall and a young boy named Nathan came running to me. He said something about saving his life. I noticed something was wrong with his left eye and his speech. He must have had some sort of stroke. I asked him to repeat what he had said while I recorded it on my iPhone. He sweetly said, "My name is Nathan, and you saved my life. I tell you!" I enquired what he meant. He said that he can now run and when he swims, he will not drown. I asked him what he wanted to say to Jesus. He sweetly said, "Thank you, Lord Jesus".

Nathan was partially healed, yet he was grateful to both me who prayed with him, and to the Lord Jesus who healed him.

Notice he said, "You saved my life". He linked healing and salvation. It must have been that the Holy Spirit was working in his heart. Healing is salvation and an attitude of gratitude.

Amen, thank you, Lord Jesus!

Regina is healed from the effects of a stroke

A woman came for prayer. I asked her "What do you want Jesus to do for you?" She said that all her side was numb, and it had been like that for two years. As we were praying, I asked her if she would mind if I pinched her leg. She didn't. So, I pinched her and said, "Do you feel that?" She shook her head and said, "It's numb, it's numb". We continued to pray and asked the Father to heal her. In prayer we reflected on Jesus' wounded legs and side. Then I asked if I could pinch her again which I did and then she said, "Yes, yes I can feel it, I can feel it". Then she got up and gave her testimony in her language. After that, I asked somebody to take her outside and record it in English:

"On the left side (of my body), my hand and my leg have been numb for two years, and today I praise the Lord for He has saved me from the pain I've been bearing. Thank you, Lord, for healing me, thank you Jesus. My name is Regina, and I am from Mount Hagen, Papua New Guinea."

Here also Regina used the word 'saved': "saved me from the pain". The Gospel is therapeutic. It is Jesus' love that heals us. When the good news is preached it brings about salvation in people's lives.

Bevlyn finds a husband

During the conference, a young woman came up to me and said, "It's me, Bevlyn". I had met Bevlyn the year before. I told her, "You're looking radiant, you look beautiful". She said, "You prayed for me to get married and I did, and now I am with a child". The following day she introduced me to her husband, Peter.

My wife Barbara and I have prayed with and for people to find their partner in life, and we encourage them to pray themselves. In our experience, a number of them have married.

After I returned to Australia, I sent a message to Peter, asking when the baby was due. He replied that Bevlyn had the baby on 11 November. I asked what name they have given her, and he texted back that they hadn't given her a name yet. "We want you to give her a name," he added. After hesitating for a while, I suggested the name Lucy and I assured them that I would not be offended if they didn't use that name. It was up to them, the parents, to name her. They came back and said, "Her name will be Lucy so that every time we call her we will remember you". On 26 November, their wedding anniversary, Lucy was baptised.

The Lord is always mindful of our needs. He promised "Ask and it shall be given you," (Matthew 7:7).

"Those who are in truth His disciples, receiving grace from Him, do in His name perform [miracles], so as to promote the welfare of other men, according to the gift which each one has received from Him. For some do certainly and truly drive out devils, so that those who have thus been cleansed from evil spirits frequently both believe [in Christ], and join themselves to the Church. Others have foreknowledge of things to come: they see visions, and utter prophetic expressions. Others still, heal the sick by laying their hands upon them, and they are made whole," (*Against Heresies*, St Irenaeus of Lyons (120-202), a Father of the Church).

29

From Islam to atheism, then God spoke to him in his own language!

"My sheep hear my voice. I know them, and they follow me. I give them eternal life, and they will never perish. No one will snatch them out of my hand,"
(John 10:27-28).

Two weeks before Christmas, 2013, a friend introduced me to an Iranian refugee. His name is Alex. Now 30 and raised in a Moslem family, while in his mid-twenties Alex had declared he did not believe in any God. I invited him for a coffee and a chat. Being an atheist, he did not want to talk about God.

"I don't need God, I need a friend," he said to me. "I will be your friend," I responded.

When I invited him to our Christmas party, he said, "I don't believe in Christmas". I replied, "Okay, just come to the party. I can introduce you to my friends". He came to a Christmas party in the Disciples of Jesus Covenant

Community. Here he mixed with many people and seemed to enjoy himself.

I then invited him to attend the 2014 Bathurst Summer School. "What is Summer School?" Alex asked. I explained that it was a one-week, live-in religious conference. He objected, "But I don't believe". I responded, "You can find out what we believe".

Because Alex was unable to cover the cost, a community member offered to pay if he was willing to participate fully, and he agreed.

On Sunday, 5 January, 2014, before the Summer School's Opening Mass; that he might better understand what would be happening, I shared with him a presentation of the basic Gospel message. I also shared with him what Jesus did at the Last Supper. During the week, he attended my lectures about 'Life in the Holy Spirit'.

In spending time with Alex each day talking about his life, I encouraged him to forgive all those who had hurt him. He attended the lectures, seminars and sharing groups, but repeated he did not believe in anything; he was an atheist!

Alex also participated in every prayer session and often wept.

During one of our chats, he said, "What did you do to my heart, Costandi?" I replied, "Jesus has your heart in His hand and is giving it a bit of a massage", meaning that God was healing him. Later I asked why he cried all the time. "Yes," he said, "I cried when I went to bed, when I was at Mass, when I was at lectures, and sometimes in my sharing group. When I heard the testimony of the girl whom Jesus healed from eczema, I cried. When everybody was speaking about God and their experiences of Him, I was crying. I don't know why I cried; my heart became soft".

At the celebration of the Sacrament of Reconciliation on Tuesday, he asked me what he should do. I suggested he go forward, tell his story to one of the priests, seek his advice and ask for a blessing. Alex shared how he stated to the priest, "I don't believe. I didn't even see (experience) anything, but I came here to find something".

The priest said, "Keep searching; if you have come here to find out about God, keep searching". The next day as we chatted, he cried and said he did not believe. I replied, "Why don't you say to God, 'God, if you exist, show me'".

During the prayer and praise session that evening, he was sobbing uncontrollably, and asked one of those with him to, "Tell Costandi that I believe in his God!" Upon asking what had happened, he told me, "God spoke to me in my language". I asked what God said to him. Alex replied that God said, "You are welcome!"

A few of us took him out of the hall where we hugged, welcomed and comforted him. Then we returned to the session to hear the testimonies and the message for that evening. There was a call for people to commit to follow Jesus.

I was on a prayer team for anyone who wanted to receive prayer or make a commitment. Alex came to me and said "Yes" to the question of "Was he ready to give his life to Jesus?"

Then I asked the following questions: "Alex, do you reject Satan and all wrongdoing?

Alex, do you believe that Jesus is the Son of God, that he died to free us from our sins and that he rose that we may have life to the full?

Alex, do you believe that God has forgiven you because Jesus died for you?"

To all these questions, Alex replied with a definite "Yes".

Then I asked him: "Alex, will you follow Jesus and obey him as your Lord, as your leader, as your God?" To this, he answered, "Yes, yes, yes!" and burst out sobbing.

I was sure that Alex understood these questions and the implication of the decision he made because he was in my lectures. I made sure they were explained fully.

The next morning I asked Alex if he'd had a good sleep. He said "Yes", but he added that he had an unusual dream. In his dream, Alex saw that he had lost the hair from the crown of his head. On his scalp, he saw a mark in the shape of a cross. I interpreted this as God placing his seal on him; he was now under the protection of the cross.

I asked Alex to share with me what had happened on Wednesday night before he burst out sobbing.

He shared:

"I asked God, 'If you exist, show me; I need to see or experience something from you. When I asked that earlier, I did not mean it, but now I mean it. I haven't seen you like everyone else. I want to see you and touch you. Am I different from everyone else? Maybe you don't want to know me?'

As people were singing, I didn't understand some words, so I spoke with Him about myself in my language. 'When I came into this world, I was like a gold ring in your hand. I was shining. I grew up, and I lost myself, I lost you and couldn't find you. I was busy with myself, with things, sometimes with sport, study, family, a girlfriend, sometimes with friends. I was lost; I didn't have time to think about you; I didn't follow your way. I was the lost one. But now you invite me; you brought me here. I need you to wash me and clean me.

Finally it's happened. God spoke to me in my language saying, 'Koosh a madi' – 'You are welcome!'"

Alex explained that the greeting used to welcome people formally is 'Koosh a madeed' whereas 'Koosh a madi' is the informal, friendly way of saying, 'Welcome to my house!' or 'Welcome to my family!'

On Thursday night when Alex asked us to pray for him for the Lord to baptise him in the Spirit, he rested in the Spirit.

Returning in conversation to the first Mass he attended on Sunday, he related to me what he experienced. He said:

"When the priest took the bread and said, 'This is My Body' and broke it, I thought, 'What does 'This is My Body' mean? Then I had a feeling that this is the Body of Jesus and the people believed it." Alex then added: "I didn't think - it came upon my heart, 'My people come here every week, they eat the bread and renew their covenant with me'. When that happened, I cried uncontrollably. It was amazing". He said to me, "You did not notice it. For seven days when we went to Mass and at Summer School, at the breaking of the bread, I cried as I remembered the feeling I had at the first Mass. The same feeling comes upon me each time I'm at Mass, sometimes before or after the breaking of the bread. No one told me it relates to the covenant; I comprehend it by my heart".

After Summer School, I met with Alex weekly and sometimes twice a week. I prepared him to receive the Sacraments of Initiation. At Easter of the same year, Alex was received into the Catholic Church. He was Baptised, Confirmed and received the Eucharist.

Since then, Alex has been a faithful Catholic and member of the Disciples of Jesus Covenant Community.

The Risen Good Shepherd is still in our midst and he continues to seek out the lost.

I heard a story of a young boy at school. The teacher gave the class an assignment to learn Psalm 23. Jonny tried hard to memorise it but couldn't. When the teacher asked him to recite it, he replied: "The Lord is my shepherd, and that's all I need to know".

"At that time Jesus said, 'I thank you, Father, Lord of heaven and earth, because you have hidden these things from the wise and the intelligent and have revealed them to infants; yes, Father, for such was your gracious will. All things have been handed over to me by my Father; and no one knows the Son except the Father, and no one knows the Father except the Son and anyone to whom the Son chooses to reveal him'," (Matthew 11:24-27).

30

Healings and a pleasant surprise at Port Moresby

"Whenever you go into a town where they make you welcome, eat what is set before you. Cure those in it who are sick, and say, 'The kingdom of God is very near to you'," (Luke 10:8-12).

My visit to Papua New Guinea in July, 2019 was amazingly rich.

Port Moresby

My first stop was Port Moresby. On Friday night, 12 July, we had a youth gathering where I spoke about baptism in the Holy Spirit and how to grow in the charismatic gifts. Many were baptised in the Holy Spirit and received the gift of tongues and other gifts.

On Saturday morning, we had a men's breakfast for 29 young men who were sponsored by the parish to encourage them to participate more fully in the life of the parish. The Disciples of Jesus Covenant Community, Port Moresby, hosted the event.

On Sunday, 14 July, we had a Healing Service as part of the Disciples of Jesus Covenant Community, Port Moresby Community General Gathering. The Lord healed many.

Healings at Port Moresby

Let me share with you these two short testimonies from two beautiful, young women:

"My name is Pauline. I had a problem with my eyesight. I couldn't see with my right eye, and with the other eye I couldn't see properly. Jesus healed me, and now I can see clearly."

"My name is Shirley. You can call me Princess Shirley." She explained that earlier I had said that God, the King of Kings, is her Father. I asked her what title we give to the daughter of a king? She answered, "Princess".

She went on to say: "I had a problem with my eyesight, it's not in my family's genes but somehow I got it. Now, after receiving prayer, I think I can see clearly".

I asked her, "You think you can see clearly, or you can see clearly?" "I can see clearly," she affirmed. "Thank you, Lord Jesus Christ, for sending this man here," Shirley added.

"Who healed you?" I asked. "Jesus! Thank you, Jesus," she added.

A Pleasant Surprise

Chatting with Anne Marie, a long-standing member of the community, I asked about a young lady named Christophilda. On my first visit to Port Moresby in 2011, we prayed with Christophilda, who had a chronic wrist injury with minimal movement. She was unable to do her housework properly as she could not apply pressure on her wrist. The doctor told her that there was nothing they could do to help her. After praying with her, she recovered full movement of her wrist. She stood up and gave her testimony while continuously rotating her wrist with no pain whatsoever.

Paul and Anne Marie Miamel and I were walking in the City Vision Shopping Centre. Anne Marie pointed to a young woman walking in our direction. It was Christophilda. What a surprise to both Christophilda and myself! She was on her lunch break, so she stopped and chatted. I asked her about her wrist. She rotated her wrist again and again. "All well," she smiled with delight.

31

A former Premier, chiefs, and businessmen rejoice in the presence of the Lord

"So, they set out and went from village to village, proclaiming the good news and healing people everywhere," (Luke 9:6).

My second stop during the 2019 visit was Mount Hagen, accompanied by Paul and Anne Marie Miamel.

In preparing for our mission, the Catholic Charismatic Renewal in Mount Hagen undertook the mammoth task of organising four conferences in four deaneries. The preparation included the erection of stages and marquees; hiring sound and music equipment, and providing community support to feed thousands of people.

Archbishop Douglas Young gave us his blessings, and Fr Robert Nolie, Spiritual Director of the Catholic Charismatic Renewal, gave us his full support. Rose Kants, president of the Catholic Women League (CWL), led the CWL conference.

Many were baptised in the Holy Spirit and received charismatic gifts. The Lord healed many from aches and pains in their bodies and many recovered their hearing and eyesight. A few who had suffered from strokes that left them partially paralysed received the ability to feel and move.

The interview was broadcast again and again all over the Western Highlands

On arrival in Mount Hagen, Paul, Anne Marie, Fr Robert Nolie and I were interviewed by Sr Maria Lilian SND of Triniti FM Radio 98.1 – Tok Pisin. The interview ran for forty-five minutes. We spoke about the grace of the baptism of the Holy Spirit, the charismatic gifts, and the gift of healings. We also talked about the role of the laity in the Church.

The interview was broadcast again and again all over the Western Highlands.

Hundreds of people attended these conferences. The chiefs, patrons and the people welcomed us in their beautiful, traditional way.

Hundreds were baptised in the Holy Spirit and received the gifts, and the Lord healed hundreds in different ways. There were many conversions, and some young men came asking to be set free from addiction to drinking and smoking.

Shortly after my return to Australia, I received a text message from former Premier, Philip Kapal, to thank me for visiting them in Mount Hagen. He said that he was thrilled and excited to have seen what happened at Fatima Community and particularly having closely witnessed Jesus healing the sick and the disabled. He described it as an experience of a lifetime. Then he added that they were looking forward to seeing the same again soon... I was pleased to sense his expectant faith.

I want to share with you a highlight from the conferences.

Blessings replace curses

"Christ redeemed us from the curse of the law by becoming a curse for us, for it is written: 'Cursed is everyone who is hung on a pole'," (Galatian 3:13).

Kiliga Conference, 17-20 July, 2019

During my previous visits to Mount Hagen, many came to be prayed with to break the curses in their lives, so I decided to give a talk on blessings and curses. Then I led them all in prayer to break inter-generational curses.

Inter-generational curses could be spiritual bondage that one generation passed down to another. Some symptoms of a generational curse are a continual negative pattern of spiritual bondage handed down from generation to generation.

On the cross, Christ broke all curses so that we might qualify for and receive His blessing.

On the day following the prayer for breaking curses, a man from the neighbouring mountain came and asked Fr Robert Nolie and I to visit them on the mountain. He wanted us to pray a blessing over the whole clan and their mountain. They believed that they were under a curse, which was now broken, and wished to receive a blessing instead.

During the lunch break, we went up the mountain where the whole clan gathered. One man spoke on behalf of them all and explained that when Catholic missionaries first arrived in the area, their great-grandfather chased them away and refused to send his children and grandchildren to the Mission School. They also believed that he planted a tree and invited an ungodly man to bless it. They believed that this and the chasing away of the priest brought curses upon them, now to the third generation. As a result, none of their men received an education, and none have been successful in life, and they have had to contend with many feuds. Hence, they asked us to pray a blessing instead.

I spoke about the importance of forgiveness and invited them to hug each other and say, "I forgive you; I love you", which they did. Then I led them to renew their baptismal vows and commit themselves to follow the Lord and his Church. When they had done that, I prayed that the Lord would bless them in every way.

One of the men came forward with a bird in his hand. He said that the bird came as we were praying. I took the bird into my hands – it was a baby bird, and I released the bird into the air, but the bird fell to the ground. Then it took off and flew away. There was great rejoicing as they saw in that a sign that the Lord has set them free.

They agreed to make 17 July an annual day of remembrance to commemorate this event. They decided to build a chapel on the spot where we gathered and to make it a house of prayer.

As I was preparing this book for publication, I received messages from Tat Pati, the son of the landowner, advising me that they are seeing changes in their area. The Western Highland Provincial Government has given them a new Lusac mill.

They are cutting timber and clearing an area to build classrooms and houses for the staff at the local Technical Secondary School. What a blessing!

Manjim High School student retreat

After the final Mass and on the way back to our accommodation, we stopped at Manjim High School and joined the student retreat. Fr Robert Nolie had agreed to close the retreat, but he invited us to minister to them. 69 students had registered for the retreat. However, people from the village joined in and so we had about 150 people there.

Fr Robert asked Paul and Anne Marie to speak on Christian marriage as the area was known for broken marriages and polygamy. They ministered beautifully.

Then I spoke about putting Jesus at the centre of our lives, led them in renewing their baptismal vows, prayed for them for healing and blessed them with the cross.

"I have never experienced anything like this in my life!"

"John answered them all, 'I baptise you with water. But one who is more powerful than I will come, the straps of whose sandals I am not worthy to untie. He will baptise you with the Holy Spirit and fire'," (Luke 3:16).

Sinsibai, Mount Hagen, PNG Conference – 26-28 July, 2019

Five parishes came together at Sinsibai for the conference. It was the largest conference with hundreds of people attending.

The power of the Holy Spirit filled the place. Hundreds gave their lives to the Lord, were baptised in the Holy Spirit and received the gifts of the Holy Spirit.

Meggie shared her experience of being baptised in the Holy Spirit:

"I was one of the participants at the conference, and I was amazed when I was baptised in the Holy Spirit – and my goodness! It was a marvellous experience because I have never experienced anything like it in my life before.

When Costandi gave us a talk on the gifts of the Holy Spirit, he said: 'In Luke 11:9-13 it says, 'Ask, and you shall receive; knock, and the door shall be opened; seek and you shall find". So, when I was praying about it, I asked the Holy Spirit if He would fill me and give me some of the gifts of the Holy Spirit. I prayed during the day and in the evening, and oh, we were full of joy, and I was one of them, and I was singing and praising God.

During the worship and praise time, I was repeating: 'Praise God', 'Thank you, God', and 'I love you, Jesus'. In the middle of what had happened, I got so excited that I thought anytime I might fall because something strange had happened. My heart was beating very fast. I was thinking, 'What is this experience now? Am I going crazy, or what is happening to me?'

A lady next to me was looking at me, but I got lost in words and continued praising God, thanking God, 'liking' Jesus. I got lost in words. My heart was really beating very fast. A new experience was happening to me, and I was speaking words I could not understand. Then everyone else stopped, but I still wanted to keep going on.

That was my experience – I was so filled with joy because one of the gifts I asked for through the Holy Spirit was the gift of tongues. I praise God, and I thank Jesus, I thank the Holy Spirit for giving me the gift of tongues."

The Joy of Evangelisation

"When you enter a town and are welcomed, eat what is set before you. Heal the sick who are there and tell them, 'The kingdom of God is near you'," (Luke 10:8-9).

Pogla (Polga) Conference, 23-25 July, 2019

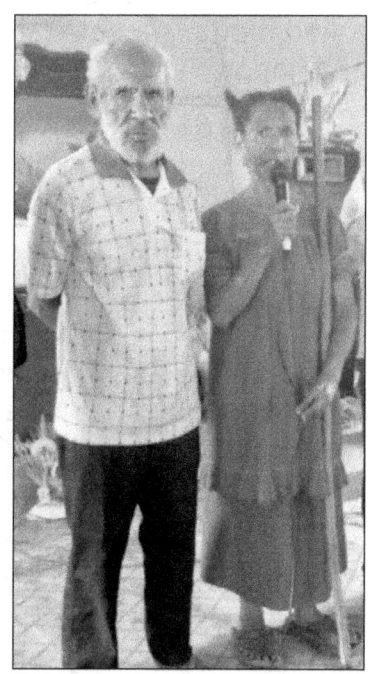

On the last day of the Catholic Charismatic Conference at Pogla, sometimes pronounced Polga, Mount Hagen, Elizabeth came to me full of joy and said that she was on her way with others to the river that morning. She saw a road leading to a house where she met Peter, a man well-known in the village. He offered her breakfast. He asked her where she was from and what brought her to this area. She told him she was from a neighbouring village and was there because she was attending a conference. She shared with him that on the previous night, the Lord baptised many in the Holy Spirit, they received the gifts of tongues and prophecy, and Jesus healed many. He was surprised that no one mentioned it to him although everyone knew that he was not well. She prayed for him and invited him to the church.

Peter was able to walk with her about one and a half kilometres to the church.

Elizabeth asked me if I would pray with Peter for his back, breathing, and hearing. I invited Paul Miamel to join us. When I saw Peter, he was bent over and leaning heavily on a stick.

After Paul, Elizabeth and I prayed with him, I asked him to stand up straight, which he instantly did. Then I asked him to breathe deeply, and he did so effortlessly. I asked him to repeat it, and he did so. He seemed relieved and happy.

I said to him, "Now you don't need your stick". He took his stick, laid it on the floor, and ran down the steps in front of the hall. He ran down the dirt pathway, to the street and back again. When he started to run, we stood there with our mouths wide open. I was afraid he was going to slip and fall as it had been raining and it was very muddy.

After the Mass, I invited Elizabeth and Peter to share their story. Elizabeth shared first. She was delighted. Oh, the joy of evangelisation!

In his sharing, Peter said that he had back and leg problems since 1982. He also had hearing problems and asthma and had not left his home for many years. Peter stood tall. He said he felt that there was nothing wrong with him anymore. Then he ran backward and forward, the full length of the hall while the onlookers cheered.

During the Conference, we spoke about evangelisation, and here we saw the fruits of evangelisation in action. Elizabeth reached out to Peter, shared with him, prayed with him, and invited him to the Mass. We prayed with him, and the Lord did the rest. He healed Peter.

People talked about the miracle, comparing this story with the man who, after being healed by John and Peter at the Beautiful Gate in the time of Jesus, went "walking and leaping and praising God," (Acts 3:8). Others exclaimed, "God truly is with us!"

"But you will receive power when the Holy Spirit comes on you, and you will be my witnesses," (Acts 1:8).

PART TWO

As I chose the testimonies to share in Part One of this book, I found that both others and I use a language that may be strange and foreign for many people in our day. Not only non-Christians but also Christians may be unfamiliar with some of the words and expressions used, such as 'baptism in the Holy Spirit', 'charismatic gifts', 'resting in the Spirit', the 'gift of tongues' and others. Hence, I decided to explain them briefly in this part of the book.

The explanations here are by no means comprehensive. They are only to give you, the reader, a brief description so you can follow the story. Many have written articles and books about the topics that follow. I encourage you to do your own research.

32

The basic Gospel message – bridge illustration

"For God so loved the world that he gave his only Son, so that everyone who believes in him may not perish but may have eternal life," (John 3:16).

Many years ago, I came across a tract illustration of the basic Gospel message. I was very impressed by it. I found it based on the sacred Scriptures, clear, concise, informative and gently challenging. It also leads the reader to a prayer of commitment. I reproduced it in a flyer and used it in street evangelisation.

Yes you can be HEALED, experience PEACE and a NEW BEGINNING

"For God so loved the world that he gave his one and only Son, that whoever believes in him shall not perish but have eternal life." (John 3:16 NIV)

How Can This Be Good News For You?

The 'Gospel' or 'Good News' is about God and us.

1. God loves us and wants to have a relationship with us. "I have loved you with an everlasting love; I am constant in my affection to you," (Jeremiah 31:3).

2. We have rebelled against God and broken off that relationship. "For the wages of sin is death," (Romans 6:23). We suffer from loneliness, isolation, depression, anxieties, insecurities, lack of direction, meaninglessness, fear, suspicion, mistrust and exploitation.

3. "But God shows his love for us in that while we were yet sinners Christ died for us," (Romans 5:8).

"By his wounds, we are healed," (Isaiah 53:5).

4. To make this good news ours, you and I must *ask* Christ to be our *forgiver* and *leader*. "If you confess with your mouth that Jesus is Lord and believe in your heart that God raised him from the dead, you will be saved," (Romans 10:9).

Do you believe that Jesus paid for your sins? Are you willing to ask God's *forgiveness* and to follow Jesus as your *leader*?

If your answers to these three questions are yes, then you can pray the following prayer, receive healing, forgiveness for all your sins, and begin a new life:

> Lord Jesus Christ, I want to belong to you from now on. I want to be freed from the dominion of darkness and the rule of Satan, and I want to enter into your kingdom and be part of your people. I will turn away from all wrongdoing, and I will avoid everything that leads me to wrongdoing. I ask you to forgive all the sins that I have committed. I offer my life to you, and I promise to obey you as my Lord. I thank you, Jesus, I love you, Lord Jesus, I praise you, Jesus.

Rejoice in the Lord always!

"They accepted what he said and were baptised... These remained faithful to the teaching of the apostles, to the brotherhood, to the breaking of bread and to the prayers," (Acts 2:41-42).

The good news according to the prophet Isaiah

Let us go to the good news as prophesied by the prophet Isaiah eight hundred years before Christ. In verses 3-6 we read: "He was despised, the lowest of men, a man of sorrows, familiar with suffering, one from whom, as it were, we averted our gaze, despised, for whom we had no regard.

Yet ours were the sufferings he was bearing, ours the sorrows he was carrying, while we thought of him as someone being punished and struck with affliction by God.

Whereas he was being wounded for our rebellions, crushed because of our guilt; the punishment reconciling us fell on him, and we have been healed by his bruises."

I encourage you to read the full text of Isaiah 53:1-12 and reflect on it.

33

Jesus our healer

"All I want is to know Christ and the power of his resurrection," (Philippians 3:10).

Who is Jesus, and why does He continue to heal today?

The name 'Jesus'. In Luke's Gospel, Luke tells us "The angel Gabriel appeared to Mary and said, 'You are to conceive and bear a son, and you must name him Jesus'," (Luke 1:32).

The word 'Jesus', or 'Yeshua' in Aramaic, means 'Yahweh is salvation'.

Why was the child to be called Jesus?

Matthew, in his Gospel, gives us the explanation that the angel gave Joseph:

"But just when he had resolved to do this, an angel of the Lord appeared to him in a dream and said, 'Joseph, son of David, do not be afraid to take Mary as your wife, for the child conceived in her is from the Holy Spirit. She will bear a son, and you are to name him Jesus, for he will save his people from their sins'. All this took place to fulfil what had been spoken by the Lord through the prophet: 'Look, the virgin shall conceive and bear a son, and they shall name him Emmanuel', which means, 'God is with us'," (Matthew 1:20-23).

This child is Emmanuel, which means 'God is with us' and 'he is the one who is to save his people from their sins'.

Often when people think of salvation they think of death and after death. They think that salvation is just going to heaven after we die. However, Jesus came to reconcile us to the Father and restore our humanity to what the Father intended it to be from the beginning.

When Jesus went about healing the sick, opening the eyes of the blind and setting the captives free, he was fulfilling his mission of salvation. Jesus came to save us from sin and the effects of sin, which include sickness, disease, weakness, loneliness, isolation, anxiety, fear, and mistrust.

'Jesus is our healer' is another way of saying 'Jesus is our saviour'.

Jesus' mission

Jesus conceived his mission as follows:

"The Spirit of the Lord is upon me because he has anointed me to bring good news to the poor. He has sent me to proclaim release to the captives and recovery of sight to the blind, to let the oppressed go free, to proclaim the year of the Lord's favour," (Luke 4:18-19).

Yes, Jesus came to heal the broken-hearted and to set the captives free. The healings and the miracles that Jesus performed and continues to perform are his very mission.

People were being saved, and are being saved today.

Luke 17:19 is translated: "Then he said to him, 'Get up and go on your way; your faith has made you well'," (New Revised Standard Version), or "And then he said to the man, 'Stand up and go on your way. Your faith has saved you'," (New Jerusalem Bible).

Healings, miracles, signs and wonders are salvation or symptoms of salvation!

"And he answered them, 'Go and tell John what you have seen and heard: the blind receive their sight, the lame walk, the lepers are cleansed, the deaf hear, the dead are raised, the poor have good news brought to them'," (Luke 7:22).

Christ's saving work involves those already completed, on-going, and future saving activities.

The miracles of Jesus are not to be seen only as 'proofs' of his divinity or as 'guarantees' that his teachings were from God. Instead, we are seeing that the healing acts of Jesus were themselves the message that he had come to set us free.

Jesus' earthly ministry made salvation a present reality for His generation.

I like the way Francis MacNutt explains salvation:

"What does it mean? What does Jesus save me from, and how does it affect my life? In traditional terms, Jesus saves us from personal sin and from the effects of original sin, which include ignorance, weakness of will, disoriented emotions, physical illness, and death. Some of this freedom will unfold only after our physical death. But even now the process has begun: 'The kingdom of God is at hand'. Jesus wants to free us from physical sickness – from all the sickness that destroys or lessens our humanity – in order to give us new life, a new relationship of love and union with His Father.

This is the astounding message of the good news. The danger is, and always has been, that we let this news remain a doctrine, a truth to be believed."[1]

Jesus gave his disciples the power to heal when he sent them out to preach

"Then, Jesus called the twelve together and gave them power and authority over all demons and to cure diseases, and he sent them out to proclaim the kingdom of God and to heal," (Luke 9:1-2).

"After this, the Lord appointed seventy others and sent them on ahead of him in pairs to every town and place where he himself intended to go," (Luke 10:1).

"He gave them the following instructions: Whenever you enter a town, and its people welcome you, eat what is set before you; cure the sick who are there, and say to them, 'The kingdom of God has come near to you'," (Luke 10:8-9).

Jesus was simply giving them the very same power to preach the message of good news that he taught.

That message contained the power of God to heal our sick humanity from its miserable state.

"Go out to the whole world and proclaim the good news... these are the signs that will be associated with believers: in my name, they will cast out devils; they will pick up snakes in their hands and be unharmed should they drink deadly poison; they will lay their hands on the sick, who will recover," (Mark 16:15-19).

---

[1] *The Word Among Us magazine, 'Jesus Saves – And Heals' by Francis MacNutt.*

Jesus combined both preaching and healing in his proclamation of the Gospel. The early apostles did the same.

The apostles also saw healings as salvation. When Peter and John were questioned after healing the blind beggar, Peter replied: "There is salvation in no one else, for there is no other name under heaven given among mortals by which we must be saved," (Acts 4:12).

Today, as in the early Church, we still need to be made whole. The Lord continues to heal and to save.

Through the Church, his Body on earth, by the Sacraments and simple prayers with expectant faith, Jesus continues to make salvation and healing a present reality in our days.

It is true; not all receive healing in the way we expect. Some healings will only take place after our physical death or when Christ comes again. However, many are healed here and now. Many more are saved as we obey the command of our Lord to proclaim the good news and heal the sick.

34

How do we understand baptism in the Holy Spirit?

"I baptise you with water for repentance... He will baptise you with the Holy Spirit and fire,"
(Matthew 3:11).

At the core of the Catholic Charismatic Renewal is the 'grace of Pentecost', also known as baptism in the Holy Spirit.

While not a theological statement, the US Bishops' Ad Hoc Committee defines baptism in the Holy Spirit this way:

"As experienced in the Catholic Charismatic Renewal, baptism in the Holy Spirit makes Jesus Christ known and loved as Lord and saviour, establishes or re-establishes an immediacy of relationship with all those persons of the Trinity, and through inner transformation affects the whole of the Christian's life. There is new life and a new conscious awareness of God's power and presence. It is a grace experience which touches every dimension of the Church's life: worship, preaching, teaching, ministry, evangelism, prayer and spirituality, service and community. Because of this, it is our conviction that baptism in the Holy Spirit, understood as the reawakening in Christian experience of the presence and action of the Holy Spirit given in Christian initiation, and manifested in a broad range of charisms, including those closely associated with the Catholic Charismatic Renewal, is part of the normal Christian life."

For more information, visit: www.nsc-chariscenter.org

(The following is an article I wrote that was first published in 'The Melkite', the Journal of the Melkite Catholic Eparchy of Australia and New Zealand, 2011, Issue 13).

I experienced baptism in the Holy Spirit in 1972. Its impact on my life was tremendous and since then I have prayed with hundreds of people for baptism in the Holy Spirit and have seen many lives empowered.

In this submission, I do not intend go into how the term 'Baptism in the Holy Spirit' is used in sacred Scripture or what it means to Christians from other denominations or what others have said about it. Not that I am unaware of all that or I consider it unimportant, but I leave it to those who are more proficient than I in those areas. I simply want to relate my observations and state what I think baptism in the Holy Spirit is. I want to describe:

The effects of baptism in the Holy Spirit on people's lives

The impact of baptism in the Holy Spirit on the Church

What baptism in the Holy Spirit is, as I understand it

How to encourage people to be open to baptism in the Holy Spirit

Should we call it something else?

The effects of baptism in the Holy Spirit on people's lives

Observing the effect of baptism in the Holy Spirit on people's lives, one may notice the following effects.

I list the effects in four groupings, three of which as they relate to the Sacraments of Initiation. The fourth I relate to the free action of the Holy Spirit.

I relate the first group to the Sacrament of Baptism.

In the Sacrament of Baptism, our sins are washed away. We receive the Holy Spirit and become sons and daughters of God thus members of his family, the Church. The Holy Spirit comes to sanctify us.

Following baptism in the Holy Spirit, people discover His power for sanctification. They become conscious of the presence of the Holy Spirit within their lives and of his action eliminating sin and bringing their lives into order. Some people experience being set free from habitual sins. As they cooperate with the Holy Spirit, they begin to appreciate the power of the cross of our Lord Jesus Christ, a power that exceeds any resources available to us left to our own. Not that the sinful tendencies of one's personality are eradicated, but they discover the authority and power of the Holy Spirit to live a life worthy of the One who called them. They experience peace and joy and grow in the fruits of the Holy Spirit (see Galatians 5:22).

They discover their divine sonship as adopted sons and daughters of the Father, and that He delights in them. Some may even feel overwhelmed with the presence of God. They may feel loved and affirmed by the Father. As a result, they experience being set free from low self-esteem and fear of rejection.

They come to know Jesus in a personal way and experience his Lordship and Majesty. They find a desire to put their life in order and live a holy life. Spending time with the Lord in prayer becomes a joy, something to which they look forward. In addition to set prayers, they discover spontaneous prayer, praying from the heart to the Lord, sharing with Him their fears, disappointments, praying for their needs, and even their wants. Many receive the gift of praying in tongues, which enables them to pour out their heart to the Lord without filtering their prayers through the intellect. Many experience a desire to read sacred Scriptures as it becomes alive to them.

The second group I relate to the Sacrament of Confirmation.

What happened to Jesus gives us a good insight into the Sacrament of Confirmation. Following his baptism in the Jordan River, and while Jesus was at prayer, the Holy Spirit descended on Him in the form of a dove and the voice of the Father bore witness to Him as his beloved Son. The Holy Spirit led Jesus into the desert to be tempted by the devil; then He returned victorious and began his public ministry. In the Sacrament of Confirmation, the Holy Spirit comes to empower us to bear witness to Christ and to launch us on our mission.

Following baptism in the Holy Spirit, people experience a fulfillment of the Lord's promise in Acts 1:8: "You shall receive power when the Holy Spirit comes upon you and you shall be my witnesses". They experience the release of the power they had received when the Holy Spirit came upon in the Sacrament of Confirmation.

This baptism in the Holy Spirit enkindles in people the desire to tell others about their relationship with Jesus Christ. They now have a story to tell. Some people receive charismatic gifts of teaching and preaching with conviction, a conviction comes from their personal experience and the witness of the Holy Spirit in their hearts. Some people receive other charismatic gifts such as the gift of prophecy. There are others – intercession, music, service, giving, helps and hospitality, to name a few. These gifts prove very effective aids to evangelisation.

Some are led to pray with others for healings, for freedom from addictions and deliverance from evil and for other needs, or for baptism in the Holy Spirit.

Those who are baptised in the Holy Spirit discover the gifts that He allocated to them. This sometimes leads them into a ministry. They discover their role in the Body of Christ (see Romans 12:6-8).

The third group I relate to the Sacrament of the Eucharist.

In the Sacrament of the Eucharist, the Holy Spirit unites us more fully to Christ and His Body, the Church.

After baptism in the Holy Spirit many experience thirst and hunger for the Word of God and the Eucharist. They discover a desire to attend Mass more often as they long to be more united with the Lord. They look forward to receiving Jesus in the Eucharist. Giving and receiving the sign of peace at Mass fills them with joy.

Many experience a thirst for Christian fellowship and are drawn to share their lives in vibrant Christian communities and in following a way of life.

The fourth group I relate to the free action of the Holy Spirit.

The Holy Spirit blows wherever He wills. He does not act only in the Sacraments but also in a spontaneous or charismatic way. Some experience the grace of baptism in the Holy Spirit even when they have not received the Sacraments, as in Acts 1:4-5. I have come across some who were baptised in the Holy Spirit outside the Catholic Church. When they were drawn to the Catholic Church, they received the Sacraments of Initiation. Others were baptised in the Holy Spirit in their own prayer time even before they heard of the Charismatic Renewal or baptism in the Holy Spirit. Others that came to be baptised in the Holy Spirit found themselves healed physically or emotionally as well as spiritually, even though they were not seeking to be healed and nor were they prayed with for healing.

Not all people receive all the effects mentioned above or receive all at once. They come to different people at different times subsequent to their experience of baptism in the Holy Spirit.

The impact of baptism in the Holy Spirit on the Church

The fruits of this grace of baptism in the Holy Spirit are not only evident in the lives of those who have experienced it but also in the formation of prayer groups, communities and ministries such as music ministry and ministries for educating children in the faith. It is also seen in the development of evangelisation programs, schools and conferences. The fruits are also evident in the development of formation programs for adults, youth ministries, charitable works and outreaches. We also see its fruits in the establishment of consecrated religious orders for men and women and the vocational call of men into the priesthood. We see the fruits of the Holy Spirit reinvigorate the vocations of those who have embraced religious life and priesthood when they are baptised in the Holy Spirit.

What is baptism in the Holy Spirit?

Baptism in the Holy Spirit is the grace from God that believers experience in a tangible way when they surrender their lives to him and ask for it with expectant faith. It 'brings to life' the graces they have received in the Sacraments of Initiation that have remained dormant in them. Baptism in the Holy Spirit is also experienced as a 'new coming' of the Holy Spirit that anoints believers with power and authority to manifest a certain gift, exercise a ministry or a role in the Church.

How to encourage people to open up to the grace of baptism in the Holy Spirit?

The way we prepare people for baptism in the Holy Spirit is very important and is followed up.

We have found that the Life in the Spirit seminars are a very effective tool to encourage people to receive baptism in the Holy Spirit. However, I wish to highlight some points and make some clarification.

A good, concise explanation of the basic Gospel message is essential: God loves us. Sin separated us from God and resulted in the mess we are in. Jesus has redeemed us by dying on the cross for us and by rising from the dead. We need to accept Jesus' forgiveness and promise to follow him as our Lord. When We do this, we will come to know Him in a personal way. Through Him we are given a new relationship with the Father in the Spirit.

Explain the Catholic understanding of salvation as being past, present and future. We are saved, being saved, and will be saved.

Explain the effect of baptism in the Holy Spirit on peoples' lives and how in relates to the Sacraments of Initiation (see above). We emphasise that they have already received the Holy Spirit in the Sacraments of Initiation and that they are sons and daughters of God, princes and princesses in the Kingdom of God, and co-heirs with Christ.

Invite people to receive baptism in the Holy Spirit by surrendering their lives to Him. They do so by:

(a) Repenting of their sins and committing themselves to follow Jesus as His disciples. Those who have received the Sacrament of Baptism are invited to renew their baptismal vows. If they are Catholic, they are also encouraged to celebrate the Sacrament of Reconciliation; and

(b) By asking with expectant faith for the Lord to baptise them in the Holy Spirit.

Following the renewal of their baptismal vows, we pray a prayer of thanksgiving for their faith and ask Jesus to free them from all evil.

Then, we invite them to say a prepared prayer requesting Jesus to baptise them in the Holy Spirit and to give them the gift of prophecy (1 Corinthians 14:1), of praying in tongues, to ask specifically for any gifts that the Lord has placed on their hearts and to ask for any other gift that He may wish to give them.

The reason we encourage them to ask for the gift of praying in Tongues is precisely because it is a gift of prayer. Whilst all the other gifts are primarily for the community, the gift of praying in tongues is for the person's own edification (see 1 Corinthians 14:4), even though the gift of speaking in tongues together with the gift of interpretation of tongues is for the benefit of the community. Also by yielding to the gift of tongues, the person learns how to surrender their whole life to the Lord. They learn that growing in the Spirit is not a matter of striving by their own efforts but by surrendering to the Lord. However, we make it clear that being baptised in the Holy Spirit does not depend on receiving the gift of tongues or any other gift. We ask in faith in the Lord's promise that the Father would give the Spirit to anyone who would ask him (Luke 11:13). We ask in expectant faith and we receive in faith. Not always do we see tangible evidence of our prayers being answered but we continue to believe that the Lord has heard us and has granted our request.

When we pray with people, we do so by the laying on of hands. This is a sign of our fraternal love, unity and solidarity with the person. We make it clear that it is the Lord and not ourselves who sends the Holy Spirit. Jesus is the One who baptises with the Holy Spirit. Our role is to pray for them and with them, calling on the Holy Spirit to come.

Follow up

We make it clear that the experience of baptism in the Holy Spirit in only the beginning. For most people the full life in the Spirit begins with baptism in the Holy Spirit. On-going teaching and formation are essential for their transformation and growth. Exercising their gifts and taking up their roles in building the Body of Christ are the only ways to fulfil God's purpose in baptising them in the Holy Spirit.

Should we call baptism in the Holy Spirit something else?

Some people point out that the term baptism in the Holy Spirit can create confusion with the Sacrament of Baptism since the Sacrament of Baptism is both a baptism in water and the Holy Spirit. This is true. The solution, however, is not in changing the title but in explaining that there is a relationship between the two. This could be to the advantage of both; those have received this grace and those who have not yet received it. As for those who have received it, it reminds them that they are incorporated in the Church the Body of Christ not by a charismatic grace but by the Sacrament of Initiation; that God is faithful to his promises, His Church, its Sacraments and institutions and has given them this grace of baptism in the Holy Spirit to render them more fruitful. It can also be of value to those who have not yet received this grace in that it challenges them to fan into flames the gifts they have received in the Sacraments and not let them lay dormant. It challenges them to open themselves up to the grace that God is giving for our times. The outpouring of the Spirit is what God is doing. We receive that outpouring in baptism in the Holy Spirit. Baptism in the Holy Spirit is a stirring that causes the infusion of the Holy Spirit in our lives as when one stirs the sugar in a cup of tea or coffee to sweeten it. It renders the graces we have received in the Sacraments more fruitful.

For those who have received baptism in the Holy Spirit and have not yet been incorporated into the Body of Christ through the Sacraments, they have the instruction of Peter on the day of Pentecost, "Be baptised in the name of Jesus," (Acts 3:38). They also have the example of the household of Cornelius who received the Holy Spirit before they were baptised. "Can anyone withhold the water for baptising these people who have received the Holy Spirit just as we have?" (Acts 10:47). Having received this grace cannot be interpreted as rendering the Sacraments superfluous.

35

The charismatic gifts

"Pursue love and strive for the spiritual gifts,"
(1 Corinthians 14:1).

The word 'charismatic' stems from the Greek *'charismata'*. The noun 'charis' means grace and the verb 'charisma' is to give freely. Then the 'charismata' are graced gifts.

Then the charismatic gifts are special gifts of a non-material sort, freely conferred by the grace of God on individual Christians. They may also be aptitudes - that is natural gifts, empowered and set free by the Holy Spirit.

They are gifts, not rewards or wages that you earn. They are not prizes or badges given for individual merits. They are gifts freely given to us out of the Holy Spirit's generosity.

They give the Christian the power and opportunity to serve and to perform works (implies energies or effects);

that is activities or results produced by imparted spiritual energy. They are also manifestations of the Holy Spirit who Himself is the gift of the Father (1 Corinthians 12:5-7).

The purpose of the charismatic gifts

The purpose of the charismatic gifts may be summarised as follows:

1. To manifest the power of God in the body of Christ on earth (1 Corinthians 14:25).

2. To help in carrying out the great commission to evangelise the whole world, (Acts 14:8-18; Acts 16:16-18).

3. To educate or teach and perfect the Church (1 Corinthians 14:3, 12, 26).

4. To affect the deliverance of God's people (Luke 1: 74-75).

In summary: for the common good (1 Corinthians 12:7).

There are four key holy Scripture passages on the charismatic gifts. You may wish to read and reflect on the following:

- 1 Corinthians 12, 13 and 14
- Romans 12:1-8
- Ephesians 4:1-16 explained
- 1 Peter 4:7-11

A burning reality today

Cardinal Joseph Ratzinger, then Prefect for the Congregation for the Doctrine of the Faith, wrote the foreword to a book by Cardinal Suenens, who was at that time Pope St John Paul II's delegate to the Charismatic

Renewal. Cardinal Ratzinger commented on the post-Vatican II period, stating: "At the heart of a world imbued with a rationalistic scepticism, a new experience of the Holy Spirit suddenly burst forth. And, since then, that experience has assumed a breadth of a worldwide Renewal movement. What the New Testament tells us about the charisms – which were seen as visible signs of the coming of the Spirit – are a burning reality today."[1]

The water of the river gives joy to God's city

From 'A Treatise on the Psalms' by Saint Hilary of Poitiers, *Office of Readings*, Saturday of Week 25 in Ordinary Time:

"The river of God is in full spate; you have provided their food, for so you have prepared it...

We who are reborn through the Sacrament of Baptism have the greatest joy, as we perceive within us the first stirrings of the Holy Spirit, as we begin to understand mysteries; we gain knowledge of prophecy, speech full of wisdom, security in our hope, gifts of healing, and dominion over the devils made subject to us. These gifts, like drops of liquid, permeate our inner self, and so beginning, little by little, produce fruits in abundance.

It is one and the same Spirit who does all this; he gives a different gift to each person, as he wishes."

---

[1] Joseph Cardinal Ratzinger, 'The Ratzinger Report', page 151. NB. Cardinal Ratzinger is now Pope Emeritus Benedict XVI.

36

Faith and the gift of faith

"Now faith is the assurance of things hoped for, the conviction of things not seen," (Hebrews 11:1).

Christian faith is a response to God's revelation of Himself and His plan.

Faith is that energy, given to us by God by which we yield to God's self-revelation. Or it is the power that God gives us by which we accept what He has done for and in us in Jesus.

Faith is a work of God in us. Our work is to assent to it and to act upon it.

Christians do not believe in faith – they believe in God – Father, Son and Holy Spirit.

Christian faith is not a blind leap or an arbitrary act of the will.

Christian faith has its foundation.

Christian faith relies on:

1. God's universally binding promises.

Examples:

God promised to give His Holy Spirit to those who ask of Him. "If you then, who are evil, know how to give good gifts to your children, how much more will the heavenly Father give the Holy Spirit to those who ask him!" (Luke 11:13).

God promised to forgive the sins of those who confessed their sins. "If we confess our sins, he who is faithful and just will forgive us our sins and cleanse us from all unrighteousness," (1 John 1:9).

God promised to give eternal life to those who believe in Jesus. "For God so loved the world that he gave his one and only Son, that whoever believes in him shall not perish but have eternal life," (John 3:16).

2. What we know about God because of what he has revealed about himself.

3. The promptings of the Holy Spirit.

We can know God's desires through the prompting of the Holy Spirit. The Spirit may lead a person to talk to a stranger on the bus. Or, to pray for the healing of someone's headache. Faith is to respond to such promptings.

Kinds of faith

Believing faith means to accept the fundamental doctrinal truths of Christianity.

Such faith is essential, but it is not sufficient.

"You believe that God is one: You do well. Even the demons believe and shudder," (James 2:19).

Trusting faith is the belief that God is good. He loves His people and He cares for them always. A person with trusting faith not only assents to a creed, but he also entrusts his life into God's hands.

Such faith is also essential, but there is more that God desires.

Expectant faith reaches out to Jesus and expects Him to act in a specific situation.

Expectant faith is to look to Jesus for specific help, to reach out and touch the fringe of His garment, to call to Him and anticipate an answer.

"Ask, and it will be given you; search, and you will find; knock, and the door will be opened for you. For everyone who asks receives and everyone who searches finds, and for everyone who knocks, the door will be opened. Is there anyone among you who, if your child asks for bread, will give a stone? Or if the child asks for a fish, will give a snake? If you then, who are evil, know how to give good gifts to your children, how much more will your Father in heaven give good things to those who ask him," (Matthew 7:7-11).

The gift of faith

The gift of faith is a gift that the Holy Spirit gives freely – mountain-moving faith.

This gift is a sudden surge, usually in a crisis, to confidently believe without a doubt that as we act or speak in Jesus' name, it shall come to pass. It is the wonder-working faith that Jesus said can move mountains (Matthew 17:20, 21:21 and Mark 11:22-24).

"Whoever believes in me will perform the same works as I do myself, he will perform even greater works, because I am going to the Father. Whatever you ask for in my name I will do, so that the Father may be glorified in the Son. If you ask for anything in my name, I will do it," (John 14:12).

The power of faith transcends man's strength

From *The Instructions to Catechumens* by St Cyril of Jerusalem:

"The other kind of faith is given by Christ by means of special grace. To one, wise sayings are given through the Spirit, to another perceptive comments by the same Spirit, to another faith by the same Spirit, to another gifts of healing. Now this kind of faith, given by the Spirit as a special favour, is not confined to doctrinal matters, for it produces effects beyond any human capability. If a man who has this faith says to this mountain 'Move from here to there', it will move. For when anybody says this in faith, believing it will happen and having no doubt in his heart, he then receives that grace."

37

Gifts of healings

"By the same Spirit another is given the gift of healing,"
(1 Corinthians 12:9).

Charismatic gifts of healings

This gift appears in the Greek as plural, literally translated 'charismatic gifts of healings'. The plural indicates that all healings are in each separate case a supernatural operation of the Spirit. Every healing is a special gift. In this way, the spiritually-gifted individual will always stand in a new dependence upon the divine giver. It also explains why a Christian cannot go into a hospital and administer healing to every sick person he sees. The plural also indicates the different kinds of diseases and afflictions requiring different sorts of healings.

The gifts of healings are manifestations of the Spirit whereby physical, psychological or spiritual healing or renewal occurs, which is due primarily to God's action. However, natural causes can also be active.

Types of healings

We usually divide healings into three classes:

1. Physical healing whereby the Lord remedies some disease of the body and the person, at least in this area, returns to health.

2. Psychological healing whereby some emotions or mental problems usually associated with unhappy memories or unhealthy psychological attitudes are alleviated or remedied. The healings in this area would correspond to the list of possible psychological problems.

3. Spiritual healings – whereby the Lord removes some habit of sin or temptation. The possible healings in this realm would correspond to the list of spiritual illnesses.

Often healings occur in several areas simultaneously since spiritual healing could have psychological and even physical effects. So, when spiritual healing occurs, it does affect the other two areas.

Healings are abundant in Christ's ministry, and the power to heal is communicated to his apostles even before Pentecost as a sign that the kingdom is at hand.

After Pentecost, healings occurred so abundantly that even the shadow of Peter (Acts 5:15) and the handkerchiefs touched to Paul (Acts 19:12) are instruments of this power.

In our days, healings are becoming more familiar in the life of the Church. Jesus our healer is with us always.

What is inner healing?

All of us have some need for healing. We all are affected by our fallen human condition and carry the effects of our sins. We can also bear scars from others sinning against us.

Often, we find ourselves captive or imprisoned by our hurts and bad experiences from our past. These hurts and bad experiences dictate to us how to act or react to situations in the present.

The Lord desires to heal us and set us free from these negatives and bad experiences in such a way that when we look at the memory, we experience peace rather than hurt.

Inner healing occurs when hurt areas are exposed to love based in Jesus Christ so that these past experiences have no binding or wounding effect on our inner life. They become memories as the person looks at them and experiences the peace of the Lord; or relationships which were binding or oppressing can now be looked at in peace.

Forgiveness plays a vital role in the healing process.

38

The gift of tongues

> *"For to one is given through the Spirit the word of wisdom... to another diverse kinds of tongues and to another the interpretation of tongues. All these are inspired by one and the same Spirit,"*
> *(1 Corinthians 12:8, 10-11).*

The gift of tongues is the more common of the charismatic gifts, yet often it is misunderstood. I believe it is most common because primarily it is a gift of prayer. Who of us does not need help in prayer? The other charismatic gifts are primary to building up the Body of Christ but he who prays in tongues 'edifies himself' and gives glory to God.

Tongues, a gift of prayer for an individual

As a gift of prayer, the gift of tongues is most common among charismatic people. "Those who speak in a tongue speak to God, but not to other people, because nobody understands them; they are speaking in the Spirit and the meaning is hidden," (1 Corinthians 14:2).

Tongues as a gift of prayer enables us to pray to God aloud but without having to worry about words and sentences. It allows us to pour out our hearts to the Lord praying or chatting in the Spirit. We can praise God, intercede for others, and give thanks from our hearts!

"For one who speaks in tongues speaks not to men but to God. He utters mysteries in the Spirit," (1 Corinthians 4:2).

"For if I pray in tongues my spirit is at prayer, but my mind contributes nothing," (1 Corinthians 14:14).

It is like 'baby talk'. Mum and baby communicate with vowels and syllables and noises. No one can translate what they are saying to each other, yet they relate and communicate with each other.

When we pray in tongues or sing in tongues, we give glory to God and build up ourselves as in any other form of prayer. "He who speaks in tongues edifies himself," (1 Corinthians 14:14). This means that the person builds up his Christian personality.

Praying or singing in tongues, however, should not be a cop-out or a substitute for praying in one's language, that is, with the mind.

What is my point here? "I want to pray with my spirit, and also to pray with my mind. I want to sing with my spirit and with my mind as well. If your praise of God is solely with the spirit, how will the one who does not comprehend be able to say 'Amen' to your thanksgiving? He will not know what you are saying," (1 Corinthians 14:15 -16).

Speaking in tongues can also be a gift for the community

When the Spirit urges someone to speak out loud, a message in tongues for the community, the message must be followed by interpretation so the community can understand. "That is why anybody who speaks in a tongue must pray that he may be given the interpretation," (1 Corinthians 12:13).

The gift of interpretations of tongues

When the Holy Spirit urges a person to speak in tongues to a community or a gathering, then we must wait and pray for an interpretation.

The Holy Spirit who inspires one person to give a message in tongues inspires someone else to give the interpretation.

When both gifts operate together, the effect will be similar to that of the gift of prophecy.

The interpreter, like the speaker in tongues, does not understand the tongues (1 Corinthians 14:2, 14). In other words, the gift of interpretation is not a gift of translation. It is the same Spirit who inspires the speaker in tongues, who also inspires the interpreter with the same message.

Miracles of tongues

Many people testify to situations where they were able to identify tongues as a living language or as a language that no people have spoken for centuries. Such a case is known as a miracle of tongues.

I once I heard an Australian young man praying in tongues. I noticed that he was repeating again and again "Alla rahima, Alla rahima", which is Arabic for 'God is merciful, God is merciful'. This young man didn't know that he was praising the merciful God in Arabic.

When someone identifies tongues as a living or a dead language we are reminded of Acts 2 where on the day of Pentecost many people from different nations could understand the apostles as they praised God in tongues.

The witness of the early Church

Fr George Montague SM writes, "For centuries after Paul and Luke, the Church prayed in tongues, even in the liturgy. They didn't call it tongues, they called it jubilation, though it scarcely differed from the way Paul describes the gift in First Corinthians".[1]

Jubilation, or the *jubilus*, was characteristic of both private prayer and communal prayer.

Deacon Eddie Ensley, in his book *Sounds of Wonder*, refers to several saints who spoke about jubilation. Here are some of the examples he gives:

St Augustine of Hippo says, "Where speech does not suffice... They break into singing on vowel sounds that through this means the feeling of the soul may be expressed, words failing to explain the heart's conceptions. Therefore, if they jubilate from earthly exhilaration, should we not sing the jubilation out of heavenly joy, (singing) what words cannot express".

In his Expositions of the Psalms, Augustine writes, "You already know what it is to jubilate. Rejoice and speak. If you cannot express your joy, jubilate: jubilation expresses your joy, if you cannot speak; it cannot be a silent joy, if the heart is not silent to its God, it shall not be silent to his reward.

---

[1] *Ennarationes in Psalmos 99:4, in 'Patrologia Latina', vol. 37, p. 1272.*

He who sings a jubilus does not utter words; he pronounces a wordless sound of joy. The voice of his soul pours forth happiness as intensely as possible, expressing what he feels without reflecting on any particular meaning; to manifest his joy, the man does not use words that can be pronounced and understood, but he simply lets his joy burst forth without words; his voice then appears to express a happiness so intense that he cannot formulate it".

St Jerome, the pioneer biblical scholar who translated the Bible into Latin, says of jubilation: "By the term jubilus we understand that which neither in words nor syllables nor letter nor speech is it possible to express or comprehend how much man ought to praise God".

St John Chrysostom, the best-known Church Father of this time in the East and the bishop of Constantinople, encouraged his people to sing without words. He says, "It is permitted to sing psalms without words, so long as the mind resounds within".

Isidore, the bishop of Seville, became one of the most venerated scholars of the Middle Ages. He mentions jubilation several times. For him it was a breathtaking experience. He says: "Language cannot explain... Words cannot explain... It is an effusion of the soul... When the joy of exultation erupts by means of the voice, this is known as jubilation".

Receiving the gift of tongues

We receive it in faith as any other gift from God. The Holy Spirit is a gentle spirit. He does not take over our personality or force us to do anything – not even to pray. We need to yield to Him so He can give us His gifts.

"They began to express themselves in foreign tongues," (Acts 2:4).

St Paul says, "If I pray in tongues..." I do the praying; I don't wait for the Spirit to force me. I surrender my voice, my tongue, and my mind to the Lord and I pour out my heart to Him in prayer; adoration, praise, thanksgiving, petition, intercession and supplication. This gift as any other gift is under my control.

I remember when I first received this gift, I shared about it at home. My father became worried: "What if it happened to you on the train, people would think you are getting mad". It is not something that happens to you. You decide to pray, and the Spirit gives you the utterance.

Do you need help in prayer? You may want to ask the Lord to give you the gift of tongues.

"Make love your aim; but be eager, too, for spiritual gifts," (1 Corinthians 14:1).

It is common to receive tongues when baptised in the Holy Spirit. If you wish to experience baptism in the Holy Spirit, I recommend that you participate in Life in the Spirit seminars as Pope Francis recommends.[2]

"Let us pray (in the Spirit who dwells within us).

Father of light, from whom every good gift comes,

send your Spirit into our lives

with the power of a mighty wind,

and by the flame of your wisdom

open the horizons of our minds.

Loosen our tongues to sing your praise

in words beyond the power of speech,

for without your Spirit

---

[2] *Pope tells priests: Run Life in the Spirit courses - CCRUK.org.*

man could never raise his voice in words of peace

or announce the truth that Jesus is Lord,

who lives and reigns with you and the Holy Spirit,

one God, forever and ever. Amen."[3]

Sing to God in jubilation

A commentary of St Augustine on Psalm 32, from *Pentecost Sunday Mass During the Day*.

"Praise the Lord with the lyre, make melody to him with the harp of ten strings! Sing to him a new song. Rid yourself of what is old and worn out, for you know a new song. A new man, a new covenant; a new song. This new song does not belong to the old man. Only the new man learns it: the man restored from his fallen condition through the grace of God, and now sharing in the new covenant, that is, the kingdom of heaven. To it all our love now aspires and sings a new song. Let us sing a new song not with our lips but with our lives.

Sing to him a new song, sing to him with joyful melody. Every one of us tries to discover how to sing to God. You must sing to him, but you must sing well. He does not want your voice to come harshly to his ears, so sing well, brothers!

If you were asked, 'Sing to please this musician', you would not like to do so without having taken some instruction in music, because you would not like to offend an expert in the art. An untrained listener does not notice the faults a musician would point out to you. Who, then, will offer to sing well for God, the great artist whose discrimination is faultless, whose attention is on the minutest detail, whose ear nothing escapes? When will you be able to offer him a

---

[3] From Pentecost Sunday Mass During the Day, Years A, B & C: Opening Prayer.

perfect performance that you will in no way displease such a supremely discerning listener?

See how he himself provides you with a way of singing. Do not search for words, as if you could find a lyric which would give God pleasure. Sing to him 'with songs of joy'. This is singing well to God, just singing with songs of joy. But how is this done? You must first understand that words cannot express the things that are sung by the heart. Take the case of people singing while harvesting in the fields or in the vineyards or when any other strenuous work is in progress. Although they begin by giving expression to their happiness in sung words, yet shortly there is a change. As if so happy that words can no longer express what they feel, they discard the restricting syllables. They burst out into a simple sound of joy, of jubilation. Such a cry of joy is a sound signifying that the heart is bringing to birth what it cannot utter in words.

Now, who is more worthy of such a cry of jubilation than God himself, whom all words fail to describe? If words will not serve, and yet you must not remain silent, what else can you do but cry out for joy? Your heart must rejoice beyond words, soaring into an immensity of gladness, unrestrained by syllabic bonds. Sing to him with jubilation."

39

A word of knowledge

"To each is given the manifestation of the Spirit for the common good. To one is given through the Spirit the utterance of wisdom, and to another the utterance of knowledge (words of knowledge) according to the same Spirit," (1 Corinthians 12:7-8).

A word of knowledge is one of the charismatic gifts of the Holy Spirit.

A word of knowledge is a supernatural revelation of facts past, present or future. Someone receives this revelation which he has not learned through the efforts of the natural mind. For example, Jesus knew the evil thoughts of the scribes (Matthew 9:26) and the marital history of the Samaritan woman (John 4:17-19). A word of knowledge enabled Peter to rebuke Ananias and Sapphira for their lying wickedness (Acts 5:1-9).

Receiving the gifts

Most people experience the charismatic gifts after being baptised in the Holy Spirit. These gifts are not rewards or badges, and one cannot earn them. The Holy Spirit gives them as He wills. Not for our own good only but for the common good (prayer or singing in tongues privately is an exception).

"Earnestly desire to receive these gifts," (1 Corinthians 14:1). Ask in faith, receive them and step out in faith, and exercise them.

Some think what if it is not God's will to give me a charismatic gift. It is a possibility. However, St Paul says: "Make love your aim and earnestly desire to receive these gifts," (1 Corinthians 14:1). We need to examine our motives; am I motivated by loving God and others or is it about me? If my motives are anything other than loving God and others, then I must purify my motives, humble myself and learn to serve others, then I can ask for the charismatic gifts.

"Trust in the Lord, and do good; so you will live in the land, and enjoy security. Take delight in the Lord, and he will give you the desires of your heart," (Psalm 37:3-5).

Finally let us heed the teaching of Vatican II in the *Decree on the Lay Apostolate (Apostolicam Actuositatem)*, paragraph 3 which states:

"For the exercise of this apostolate (the apostolate of the laity), the Holy Spirit who sanctifies the people of God through ministry and Sacraments gives the faithful special gifts also (1 Corinthians 12:7) allotting them to everyone according as He wills (1 Corinthians 12:11) in order that individuals administering grace to others just as they have received it may also be 'good stewards' of the manifold grace of God (1 Peter 4:10) to build up the whole body in charity (Ephesians 4:16). From the acceptance of these charisms including those which are more elementary there arises to each believer the right and duty to use them in the Church and in the world for the good of men and the building up of the Church in the freedom of the Holy Spirit who 'breathes what He wills' (John 3:8). This should be done by the laity in communion with their brothers in Christ, especially with their pastors who must make a judgement about the true nature and proper use of these gifts, not to distinguish the Spirit but to test all things and to hold what is good (1 Thessalonians 5:12, 19-21)."

Of course, one may write a whole book on the charismatic gifts and their use in the Church today. Indeed many books have been written.

If you would like to receive charismatic gifts to empower you to serve the Lord, His people and build the kingdom, I strongly recommend that you participate in a Life in the Spirit seminar. Many prayer groups and communities such as the Disciples of Jesus Covenant Community run these seminars regularly.

Pope Francis recommends the Life in the Spirit seminar

Pope Francis gave an address to the International Catholic Charismatic Renewal:

"I ask you for your important contribution to be committed to share with all in the Church the baptism you have received. You have lived this experience; share it in the Church. And this is the most important service – the most important that can be given to everyone in the Church. To help the People of God in their personal encounter with Jesus Christ, who changes us into new men and women... It would be very good to organise seminars of Life in the Spirit, together with other Christian charismatic realities, for brothers and sisters that live on the street: they also have the Spirit within that pushes them, so that someone outside will open wide the door."[1]

---

[1] www.zenit.org/en/articles/pope-s-address-to-charismatic-renewal.

Pope Francis at an international retreat for priests:

"I ask all of you, each of you, that as part of the stream of the grace of the Charismatic Renewal planning seminars of Life in the Spirit, in your parishes, in your seminaries and schools... share the baptism of the Spirit and your catechesis, because it is produced by the work [of the] Holy Spirit through a personal encounter with Jesus, which changes lives."[2]

Pope Francis gives an address on the identity and mission of the Catholic Charismatic Renewal:

"The breathing of Christians draws in the new air of the Holy Spirit and then exhales it upon the world: it is the prayer of praise and missionary outreach. Share baptism in the Holy Spirit with everyone in the Church."[3]

---

2   http://en.radiovaticana.va/news/2015/06/12/pope_francis_leads_meditation_for_international_priests/1151173
3   www.news.va/en/news/pope-seek-the-unity-which-is-the-work-of-the-holy

40

What is resting in the Spirit?

It is the power of the Holy Spirit so filling the person with a heightened inner awareness that the body's energy fades away, and they let themselves go and fall gently down. Some may feel it coming, and others feel overwhelmed and find themselves on the floor, caught up in God.

The person remains conscious but caught up in a spiritual reality. A lady described her experience, saying that it was similar to when giving birth. She said that when she was giving birth, she was caught up in that experience that she didn't care what was happening around her.

During that time of surrender the person allows God to move more powerfully and directly within a person's body, mind and spirit.

Some experience the presence of God or being loved by Him. Some may rest peacefully, and other may cry, others may laugh as they are filled with love and joy.

This is not to say that God cannot or does not bring about healing or reveal his presence intimately otherwise; indeed, he does. It is to say that, in his wisdom, God has chosen this particular means to touch this person and to bring about healing and wholeness.

It is a spiritual experience that God does not force upon anyone, and everyone can block or prevent it from happening.

Remember, though; this is a gift given to us for our greater good. People should not go seeking this or that experience. We should always seek the Lord.

Each of us is unique, and it is up to the Lord to grant us this or that experience. He does it if it is good for us and according to His timing.

41

A prayer for miracles
(Fr John Rea SM)

Several years ago a friend sent this prayer composed by Fr John Rea SM. I have been praying it regularly and often. It is a school for miracles. I learned a lot praying this prayer and I have noticed its impact on my ministry.

So here it is:

Father, in Jesus' Name, please anoint me constantly with Your Holy Spirit, that I may pray effectively for every kind of blessing. Give me, I beseech You, simple, child-like, expectant faith for miracles – some of Your own faith – the faith that moves mountains. Let me be a voice for Your creating word so that I may say, 'Let it be' and you will say, 'It is'.

Come, Holy Spirit. Where you are, there is freedom. Come, please, and free me from every limiting factor and from any sense of disqualification. Free me from slavery to self, slavery to persons other than the Three Divine Persons, slavery to things. Free me from every worldly influence.

Free me from the spirit of the age, from every vestige of scepticism and unbelief. Free me from every snare of the enemy. Redeem whatever is unredeemed in me.

Spirit of Truth, teach me signs and wonders – how to yield in faith and obedience; how to be docile to You so that these may abound, wherever I am, whatever I am doing, whether the persons I intercede for are present or absent. The charisma are Your work. You give them to each person as You will. Release signs and wonders through me, I pray. You who showed Yourself as wind and fire at the first Christian Pentecost, please re-shape me for the work by granting me deep, abiding repentance for sin, a spirit of prayer, lasting awareness of my own nothingness, and limitless compassion. Thank you, gracious and kindly Spirit of God.

Heal every physical, genetic, neurological, psychological, psychiatric, and spiritual illness, disease, and injury that I pray against. Let me see the victims healed before my eyes. I ask, too, the grace to pray for fruitfulness with and for childless couples that they may have children.

Let me pray with and for the cold, arrogant, and indifferent, with and for agnostics, atheists, sceptics, and the prejudiced; for those caught up in ideologies, in modernity and post-modernity; with and for those in cults, sects, all non-Christian religions, and see them converted to Jesus Christ.

Father, so anoint me with, and immerse me in Your Holy Spirit that wherever I am He will not only heal but break curses, destroy strongholds, deliver the demonised, resolve crises and apparently hopeless situations, convert people singly and in masses, perform every kind of miracle, suspend natural laws, and raise the dead.

I ask for habitual words of knowledge, words of wisdom, discerning of spirits, in great variety, miraculous in number, accuracy, appropriateness and effects, together with the ability to read the secrets of hearts, all leading to numerous conversions to Jesus.

Cause your signs to occur in great numbers wherever I am and whenever I pray, preach, teach, or minister in any other way. Let these miracles be an infallible means of evangelising those concerned, their families, friends, and all who learn what You do through this ministry. Grant me, too, I pray, the gifts of teaching 'miracles' and of imparting the charisma on Your behalf to others whom You call to exercise them.

I make this prayer, relying on Jesus' promise, "Truly, truly, I say to you, he who believes in me, will also do the works that I do; and greater works than these will he do, because I go to the Father. Whatever you ask in my name, I will do it," (John 14:12-13).

I commit myself, Father, always to give you all the glory, always to hold You in greatest awe. Humble me in all ministry and keep me humble. All power is Yours and all honour belongs to You. "Not to us, O Lord, not to us, but to Your Name be the glory," (Psalm 115:1). I submit myself to You totally as Your creature, Your servant, Your son/daughter, and ask You to use me to extend Your reign in the hearts of the people of our time. Here I am, Lord. Use me. In Jesus' Name, I pray. Thank You. Amen.

You may add the Litany of the Saints on the following page.

Also you may find the following prayers by Fr John helpful:

Lord, grant to your servant N... to speak Your word with all boldness, while You stretch out Your hand to heal, and signs and wonders are performed through the name of Your holy servant Jesus. Amen.

Father, I bring you N... whose deep and urgent need You know. In Jesus' Name I ask you to grant him/her the miracle that alone will fulfil that need. Please pour out Your love on him/her so that You may be glorified the more, so that Your Son's kingdom may spread, and our brother/sister is blessed with healing and all else You want to give at this time. Thank You, Heavenly Father. Amen.

Litany of the miracles and wonder-worker Saints:

Mary, conceived without sin, pray for us who have recourse to thee.

St Joseph,	Pray for us.
Angels of God,	Pray for us.
Holy Angel, my Guardian,	Pray for us.
Moses, servant of God,	Pray for us.
Joshua, son of Nun,	Pray for us.
Elijah, the Tishbite,	Pray for us.
Elisha, son of Shaphat,	Pray for us.
Philip the Evangelist,	Pray for us.
Paul of Tarsus,	Pray for us.
Gregory Thaumaturgus,	Pray for us.
St Nicholas of Myra,	Pray for us.
St Anthony of Padua,	Pray for us.
St Frances of Paola,	Pray for us.
St Rita of Cascia,	Pray for us.
St Catherine of Siena,	Pray for us.
St Vincent Ferrer,	Pray for us.
St Francis Xavier,	Pray for us.

John Francis Regis,	Pray for us.
St Therese of Lisieux,	Pray for us.
St Peter Chanel,	Pray for us.
St John Vianney,	Pray for us.
St John XXIII,	Pray for us.
St John Paul II,	Pray for us.
St Pio of Pietrelcina,	Pray for us.
St Mariam of Jesus Crucified,[1]	Pray for us.
All holy wonder-workers,	Pray for us.

---

[1] *Added by the author. Palestinian Carmelite nun of the Melkite Catholic Church, canonised on 17 May 2015.*

PART THREE

In this part of the book I would like to introduce to you bodies and ministries in the Church that I have referred to or mentioned in Part One, of which you may or may not have heard.

This information is taken from their official websites. I encourage you to visit these sites and perhaps contact them and even relate to them. They are new buds in this springtime in the life of the Church and the People of God.

42

What is the Catholic Charismatic Renewal?

The Catholic Charismatic Renewal is the outgrowth from a retreat held in February, 1967 of several faculty members and students from Duquesne University in Pittsburgh, Pennsylvania. Many of the students – though not all – experienced a movement of God's Spirit called being 'baptised in the Holy Spirit'. The professors had previously been 'baptised in the Spirit' a week or two before. God's action was also prepared for in a very human way by the students' prayerful preparation in reading the Acts of the Apostles and a book entitled *The Cross and the Switchblade*.

What happened quickly spread to graduate students and professors at the University of Notre Dame and others serving in campus ministry in Lansing, Michigan. It continued to spread so that within nearly 40 years the Catholic Charismatic Renewal had spread to over 238 countries in the world, having touched over 100 million Catholics.

As early as 1969, only two years after the Renewal started, the US Bishops investigated the fledgling movement and the Committee on Doctrine wrote that, "Theologically the movement has legitimate reasons of existence. It has a strong biblical basis. It would be difficult to inhibit the working of the Spirit which manifested itself so abundantly in the early Church".

Subsequent statements in 1975, 1984 and 1997 have been equally affirming.

The 1984 statement, *A Pastoral Statement on the Catholic Charismatic Renewal*, concluded with these words:

"We wish those in the Charismatic Renewal to know that we make our own the view of Yves Congar: 'The Charismatic Renewal is a grace for the Church'. We assure those in the Charismatic Renewal of the support they enjoy from the bishops of the United States, and we encourage them in their efforts to renew the life of the Church."

Papal approval and encouragement of the Charismatic Renewal

In 1975 Pope Paul VI greeted ten thousand Catholic charismatics from all over the world at the ninth international conference of the Renewal, saying, "The Church and the world need more than ever that 'the miracle of Pentecost should continue in history'... How could this 'spiritual renewal' not be 'good fortune' for the Church and the world?" (Another translation of 'good fortune' is 'a chance').

Pope John Paul II was also an enthusiastic supporter of the Catholic Charismatic Renewal. In 1979 soon after becoming Pope he said, "I am convinced that this movement is a sign of the Spirit's action... a very important component in the total renewal of the Church". He met with the international leaders of the Renewal on a number of occasions, and regularly sent greetings to national and international conferences on the Renewal.

Pope Benedict XVI continued this practice of his predecessor.

Pope Francis in 2019 established a new international body to replace two previous bodies, International Catholic Charismatic Renewal Service and the Catholic Fraternity. The Pope charged the new body – called CHARIS – to:

1. Share baptism in the Holy Spirit with everyone in the Church. It is the grace you have received. Share it! Don't keep it to yourselves!

2. Serve the unity of the Body of Christ, the Church, the community of believers in Jesus Christ. This is very important, for the Holy Spirit creates unity in the Church, but also diversity. The personality of the Holy Spirit is interesting: with the charisms he creates the greatest diversity, but then he harmonises the charisms in unity. St Basil says that "the Holy Spirit is harmony"; he creates harmony: harmony in the Spirit and harmony among us.

3. Serve the poor and those in greatest need, physical or spiritual. This does not mean, as some might think, that suddenly the Renewal has become communist. No, it has become evangelical, for this is in the Gospel.

Pope Francis said, "These three things – baptism in the Holy Spirit, unity in the Body of Christ and service to the poor – are the forms of witness that, by virtue of baptism, all of us are called to give for the evangelisation of the world. An evangelisation that is not proselytism but first and foremost witness – a witness of love: "See how they love one another". That was what impressed those who encountered the first Christians: "See how they love one another".[1]

---

1 http://w2.vatican.va/content/francesco/en/speeches/2019/june/documents/papa-francesco_20190608_charis.html

43

The Disciples of Jesus Covenant Community

A COMMUNITY OF DISCIPLES MOVING TOGETHER UNDER THE GRACE OF THE HOLY SPIRIT TO RENEW THE CHURCH AND EVANGELISE THE WORLD.

The Disciples of Jesus Covenant Community is a body of families, singles, priests, brothers and sisters who have come together under the inspiration of the Holy Spirit, and the grace of the Catholic Charismatic Renewal to live a common life of prayer, sharing and service.

Way of life

Members of the Disciples of Jesus Covenant Community understand themselves as being a body in and for the Church. They desire to live in deep unity and spirit with the pope and bishops, and to be loyal to the teachings of the Magisterium. They find authentic tradition in the lives and writings of the Saints and Fathers of the Church. Members have a strong sense of the Sacraments in their life.

Members of the Disciples of Jesus eventually make a life-long commitment to live together a covenant reflecting God's promise and love for His people.

History

The Disciples of Jesus Covenant Community began in Sydney in October, 1979, and, on 1 September, 1994, amalgamated with Hephzibah Covenant Community which began in Canberra, ACT, in February, 1982. The amalgamated community, which retained the name Disciples of Jesus, currently has branches in Canberra, Sydney North, Sydney South, the Blue Mountains, Melbourne, Perth, Adelaide, Hobart, Darwin, Wollongong, Denpasar (Bali), Manila (Philippines), and Port Moresby and Mount Hagan in Papua New Guinea. It now numbers about 1,100 men, women and children.

Since the early 1980s the Community has been affiliated with other covenant communities throughout the world and is a member of the Catholic Fraternity of Charismatic Covenant Communities and Fellowships which is recognised as a Private Association of the Christian Faithful of Pontifical Right.

44

Summer School of Evangelisation

This is a work of the Disciples of Jesus Covenant Community. For over 30 years, Summer School of Evangelisation has been serving the needs of young people around Australia and beyond. They come to a Summer School and walk the journey with the Disciples of Jesus Covenant Community and let God lead them along the special path he has planned for their lives.

The Summer School of Evangelisation has a central purpose – the unique encounter between each person and the living God whose great love and mercy has overflowed for all humanity from the dawn of creation. Through the resurrection of Jesus and the gift of the Holy Spirit, we are "made alive" (1 Corinthians 15:22). It is in this new life that we are able to live life to the full.

What is it?

A week-long retreat that take place in four different locations: Bathurst, Melbourne, Sydney and Perth, usually on the second week of January every year. Participants retreat into the powerful experience of the Holy Spirit, opening up possibilities for deepening faith, peace, healing, joy, freedom and passion for the Gospel of Jesus.

Journeying with others

Participants in the Summer School of Evangelisation journey with other Catholics for the week, forming a unique faith community, bonded by a common vision to seek God. They share and support each other through allocated small group time each day with those of similar ages. They also build new friendships and discover the vibrant youth and young adults in our Catholic Church.

What happens?

Presentations and lectures are given by those with formal theological training and/or extensive personal experience of faith and Christian community. Lecture topics include Scripture, Catholic teaching, evangelisation, living as a disciple, and prayer. Seminars offer a practical opportunity to experience, participate in, and question issues, methods, and vision for evangelisation in areas such as: prayer, discernment, healing, gifts of the Holy Spirit, intercession and faith in action. There are many opportunities for communal and personal prayer, including charismatic praise and worship and Mass.

45

Light to the Nations

What is it?

Young people come on pilgrimage from all around Australia, and other countries throughout the Pacific, camping under the open skies and joining in an awesome celebration of the Easter liturgies. They find Jesus in a new way, through prayer, worship, drama, music, and personal sharing.

Since 1987, the Light to the Nations Easter Youth Pilgrimage has been hosted by the Disciples of Jesus Community each alternate year.

For who?

Light to the Nations is for young people (aged 16+) and the young at heart. Families also come and join in with hundreds for this amazing experience and are most welcome!

46

The Missionaries of God's Love priests and brothers

Identity and mission

The fire of God's love

Jesus said, "I have come to bring fire to the earth and how I wish it were blazing already,". The Missionaries of God's Love exist to share Jesus' mission to bring this fire to the earth. It is the fire of God's love, burning in the heart of Jesus, which took Him to the cross. It is also the fire of the Holy Spirit poured out at Pentecost, and now experienced in a new way in the Church. The Missionaries immerse themselves in this fire through the grace of 'baptism in the Spirit', through daily meditation on the cross of Jesus, and through Eucharistic Adoration. With this fire burning within their hearts, they give all for the sake of the kingdom and, commit themselves to the spreading of the good news of God's love to the ends of the earth.

A life with Jesus

The Missionaries experience the Lord consecrating them to Himself. Each brother experiences the Lord choosing, calling, and setting him apart for the kingdom of God. Jesus calls us to be with Him and to share His way of life. He calls us into radical poverty, celibacy and obedience in imitation of Him.

History

The Missionaries of God's Love began within the Disciples of Jesus Covenant Community in Canberra in 1986, under the guidance of Fr Ken Barker. Some young men, who belonged to the Covenant Community, approached Fr Ken, expressing a call to the priesthood, but also wanting to remain part of the community. They agreed to meet weekly before the Blessed Sacrament for a year in order to listen to the Lord's direction. At the end of that time they began to share a common life together in a fraternity house, seeking to live the Gospel in a radical manner, by imitating Jesus in his poverty, and developing a strong life of prayer and brotherhood. They began to understand that their commitment to contemplative prayer, Adoration of Jesus in the Blessed Sacrament, and charismatic worship, was meant to empower them to bring God's love to others, especially to the alienated and marginalised in society.

Over the years, many men heard the call of Jesus to consecrate themselves to him and give their lives for the proclamation of the Gospel. The Lord has called us to go out on mission throughout Australia and the Asia-Pacific region.

The Missionaries of God's Love priests and brothers currently have missions in Canberra, Melbourne, Sydney, Darwin, and in Manila in the Philippines. In all of these areas we seek to bring people into a living relationship with Jesus by proclaiming the love of God through the power of the Holy Spirit. Our ministry always has a particular focus on bringing the Gospel to young people and to those who are poor or marginalised.

Charismatic

The Missionaries of God's Love are fundamentally Catholic – our life is built upon the foundation of Baptism, Confirmation and Eucharist.

We are also charismatic; our life springs from the experience of the 'baptism in the Holy Spirit'. This the grace that renews sacramental Baptism, opens one to charismatic gifts, brings one into deeper conscious relationship with Jesus as saviour and Lord, and brings personal transformation, enabling a person to yield the fruits of the Spirit in a new way.

Disciples of Jesus Community

A distinctive feature of the Missionaries of God's Love is that it is a consecrated group within a Catholic charismatic Covenant Community, the Disciples of Jesus. The Disciples of Jesus Community is a lay community located in Australia, Indonesia, Papua New Guinea and the Philippines. The community is made up of people from all walks of life, all states of life, and all stages of life. Members are dedicated to developing a Catholic way of life which is true to their baptismal calling. They seek to live out their Baptism by developing a way of life that is true to the Gospel, and by bringing the good news of Jesus to others through various works of evangelisation.

Consecrated

We are Missionaries of God's Love. We consecrate ourselves to the Lord through vows of poverty, chastity and obedience, and to offer ourselves for the preaching of the good news to the ends of the earth.

When the Missionaries take vows they call upon the fire of the Holy Spirit to empower them and they consecrate themselves to the heart of Jesus broken in love for the world, placing themselves under the mantle of protection of Mary the Mother of God, who they trust graciously intercedes for them.

Ministry Vision

We are priests and consecrated brothers together in mission, sharing in the work of evangelisation in a collaborative way with lay people. We always seek to empower the laity in their journey towards holiness and their mission to spread the good news. In return, we draw much strength and support from the lay community which is integral to our identity.

In our vows, we dedicate ourselves to the preaching of the good news of Jesus for the salvation of all men and women. We aim to lead people to a personal relationship with Jesus Christ, and to experience a new outpouring of the Holy Spirit in their lives. We also seek to help people develop their gifts and to equip them with the knowledge and skills they need in order to be able to bring the good news of Jesus to others. Wherever we go we invite people to personally experience a new release of the power of their Baptism and Confirmation through a new outpouring of the Holy Spirit. We also try to build vibrant community life so that people have a rich experience of belonging within the Church and receive the support and challenge they need to grow as followers of Jesus. We have a particular focus on reaching young people with the liberating message of Jesus. We also focus on those groups of people who are unchurched or alienated from the Church in some way.

Visit www.mglpriestsandbrothers.org

47

The Missionaries of God's Love sisters

Sisters' vision

A life with Jesus

The Missionaries of God's Love sisters experience the Lord consecrating them to Himself. Each sister experiences the Lord choosing, calling, and setting her apart for the kingdom of God. Jesus calls us to be with Him and to share His way of life. We express our response of love to God through our vows of poverty, chastity and obedience in a lifestyle of prayer, sisterhood and evangelisation.

Sisters' identity

The Missionaries of God's Love sisters exist as a consecrated group living totally and exclusively for Jesus and with Jesus.

Disciples of Jesus Community

A distinctive feature of the Missionaries of God's Love is that it is a consecrated group within a Catholic charismatic covenant community, the Disciples of Jesus. The Disciples of Jesus has branches in Australia in the cities of Canberra, Sydney, Perth, Adelaide, Melbourne, Darwin and Hobart. It also has branches in Bali (Indonesia) and Manila (Philippines). The community is made up of people from all walks of life, all states of life, and all stages of life. Members are dedicated to developing a Catholic way of life which is true to their baptismal calling. They seek to live out their Baptism by developing a way of life that is true to the Gospel, and by bringing the good news of Jesus to others through various works of evangelisation.

We are fundamentally Catholic – rooted in Baptism, Confirmation and Eucharist.

We are charismatic – springing from the experience of the 'baptism in the Holy Spirit' – a 'big grace' that renews sacramental Baptism, opens one to charismatic gifts, brings one into deeper conscious relationship with Jesus as saviour and Lord, and brings personal transformation, enabling a person to yield the fruits of the Spirit in a new way.

We are members of Disciples of Jesus Covenant Community – full membership of the community is attained by covenant, a public commitment to give one's life to the Lord under the grace, vision and mission of the community.

We are Missionaries of God's Love – full commitment as a Missionary is attained through private vows, which are solemn promises before the Lord taken in a public manner to live poverty, celibacy and obedience, and to offer oneself as a consecrated person for the preaching of the good news to the ends of the earth.

When we take vows we call upon the fire of the Holy Spirit to empower us and consecrate ourselves to the heart of Jesus broken in love for the world, and place ourselves under the mantle of protection of Mary the Mother of God, who we trust graciously intercedes for us.

The Missionaries of God's Love sisters are moving towards Canonical recognition and hope to become a religious institute.

Visit www.mglsisters.org

Conclusion

"I am with you always," *(Matthew 28:20).*

All the healings and signs and wonders witness not only to Jesus' presence with us but also to His love. It is not His power that heals us; it is His love that heals us.

So, my dear reader, I would like to share with you some key verses, to sum up, what you may keep in mind after reading this book and reflecting on the testimonies in it. I do this because, "Faith comes from what is heard, and what is heard comes through the word of Christ," (Romans 10:17).

The promise

"But you will receive power when the Holy Spirit has come upon you; and you will be my witnesses in Jerusalem, in all Judea and Samaria, and to the ends of the earth," Acts 1:8).

The promise is for all; those who are close by and those who are far away. That includes you and me: "The promise is for you and your children and for all who are far off – for all whom the Lord our God will call," (Acts 2:39).

The world loves power; fame, money, control, and so on. However, here the Lord promises us the power of love; the power of the Holy Spirit who is love. So here we are talking not about the 'the love of power', but about the 'power of love'. St Paul eloquently describes love in 1 Corinthians 13.

The Lord offers us this power for one purpose only: "You will be my witnesses".

We receive power when the Holy Spirit comes upon us. For most people, they received the power when they were first baptised. Often that power remains dormant; it just needs to be stirred up.

Receive the power

"Make love your aim; but be eager, too, for spiritual gifts, and especially for prophesying," (1 Corinthians 14:1).

Be eager for spiritual gifts. Eagerly desire spiritual gifts, longing and thirsting for them. They are the manifestations of the Spirit, and thus they are a wonderful means for evangelisation. But always check your motives. Ensure that love of God and others motivates you. If your motives are not pure, that is, if love is not what is moving you, then repent; change the way you think.

Be obedient

"And he sent them out to proclaim the kingdom of God and to heal," (Luke 9:2).

When Jesus sent the seventy, he also instructed them: "Cure the sick who are there, and say to them, 'The kingdom of God has come near to you'," (Luke 10:9).

The Lord commanded us to go and make disciples of all nations (Matthew 28:19-20), so let us follow his instruction to proclaim the kingdom and heal the sick.

Be expectant

"These signs will accompany those who believe: by using my name they will cast out demons; they will speak in new tongues; they will pick up snakes in their hands, and if they drink any deadly thing, it will not hurt them; they will lay their hands on the sick, and they will recover," (Mark 16:17-18).

The Lord is always faithful to his promises. Healing, signs and wonders will follow.

"The disciples went forth and preached the Gospel, while the Lord worked with them, confirming the word through accompanying signs," (Mark 16:20).

Commit yourself to give God all glory

All power and all honour belong to God. So, commit yourself to give God all the glory. "Not to us, O Lord, not to us, but to Your Name be the glory," (Psalm 115:1).

Glory belongs to the Father and to the Son and to the Holy Spirit.

As it was in the beginning, is now and ever shall be world without end. Amen.

For the kingdom, the power and the glory are yours now and for ever.

About the author

Costandi Bastoli was born in Jerusalem and lived there for 21 years. In November, 1969, he migrated to Australia with his family and became an Australian citizen. He completed his tertiary studies and became an Associate of the Australian Insurance Institute.

In 1972 Costandi, or Cosi, was baptised in the Holy Spirit and joined the Catholic
Charismatic Renewal movement. He served as one of the coordinators of the Catholic Charismatic Renewal in Sydney for four years. In 1979, Costandi became a founding member of the original Disciples of Jesus Covenant Community.

Costandi is married to Barbara, and they live in the Blue Mountains region of New South Wales, Australia. They have five children and seven grandchildren. Costandi is also leader of the local branch of the Disciples of Jesus Covenant Community. He has vast experience in the use of the charismatic gifts and has been active in the healing ministry for over 40 years. Costandi's ministry of leading seminars and healing rallies has stretched across Australia, Papua New Guinea and the Philippines.

Costandi has been an active director of Harvest Journeys since 1991 and has regularly led pilgrimages to the Holy Land. He is a Lieutenant Emeritus of New South Wales Lieutenancy of the Equestrian Order of the Holy Sepulchre of Jerusalem, which he founded in 1995. The popes have entrusted this Order with the care and support of the Christians in the Holy Land.

www.ingramcontent.com/pod-product-compliance
Lightning Source LLC
Chambersburg PA
CBHW070250010526
44107CB00056B/2412